General Information

Note:

All quilts in this book are made using triangle foundation grids from the Triangulations™ 2.0 disc. This software is available at your local quilt store or through Bear Paw Productions, PO Box 230589, Anchorage, AK 99523. (907) 349-7873
www.bearpawproductions.com

Introduction

I can't seem to help myself, I love triangle quilts. Large quilts, small quilts - I am really not particular about the project size. The true objects of my affection are the half square and quarter square triangle units. The construction of half and quarter square triangle units is a very comforting process when pieced using Triangulations grids.

I developed Triangulations to help ease quilters' frustration levels when sewing half square triangle and quarter square triangle units. The lowly, but ever-versatile, triangle is the most often tortured shape. Even small errors in the cutting and sewing process add up to disaster — especially when bias edges are mishandled.

Gridded triangle foundations are the answer. The fabrics are placed right sides together with a precise foundation triangle grid on top. The sewing lines are provided, eliminating the ¼" seam allowance worry while sewing the units. Cutting lines are printed on the paper foundation, ensuring consistent and accurate sized shapes.

With the Triangulations™ 2.0 disc you can now create any grid your heart desires right from the convenience of your home — any time of day or night. If you have access to a computer and printer, you're ready to go. Simply print the number of grids you need at the desired dimensions and you're ready to fly. I do realize, however, that some quilters are not equipped with a computer to utilize this fabulous quilting method. Therefore, I have included alternate cutting directions so that triangle units can be pieced for each project using traditional methods.

Basics

* All quilt patterns have been written specifically with the use of Triangulations ™ in mind. Cutting and sewing instructions reflect this. Further Triangulations instructions are on the disc.

* Alternate cutting instructions have been provided for quilters who choose traditional triangle construction methods. Look for the red box.

* Yardage is calculated on 42" wide fabric.

* Pre-wash and press fabrics using spray starch prior to cutting. Spray starch will make finger pressing much more effective.

Pressing

* FINGER PRESS!!! When using Triangulations™ grids, bear in mind that the papers have ink or toner on them. A hot, steamy iron can dislodge all of that black stuff and transfer it to your iron, ironing board and eventually to your fabric.

* Press each seam in the direction indicated by the arrow. To the best of my ability, I have tried to find the most efficient pressing for each pattern. The seams will be pressed in opposite directions as much as possible. If no pressing directions are given, press as you wish.

* A great steam iron is a wonderful tool if used judiciously! Many use the iron with too much gusto. When piecing, I finger press all seams until the block is complete. Only after the final seams are finger pressed do I press with a iron in a straight up and down motion! This prevents stretching and distortion of the block.

Split and Pinwheeled Seams

* In the pursuit of seams that oppose one another, sometimes it is beneficial to think outside of the box.

* Start with two units with opposing seams. Stitch the long seam that connect the two units.

* Pull the last two or three stitches of the seams that extend past the long seam into the 1/4" seam.

* This will allow you to split the long seam at the center; all of the seams will be rotating in the same direction and the bulk at the center will be distributed.

* A circle will be used to indicate the seams that should be split and pinwheeled.

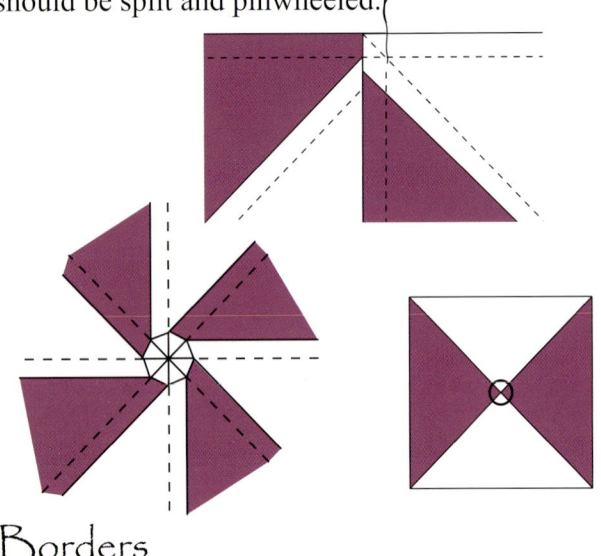

Borders

* Most border dimensions given are generous for the quilt. This allows for differences in piecing accuracy. Measure the quilt and cut the border strips to length.

* Final Borders are most effective if cut along the lengthwise grain of the fabric. If a lengthwise grain strip is suggested, cut these strips first.

Binding

* Stitch strips together on the diagonal as diagramed below. Trim seams to 1/4" and press open.

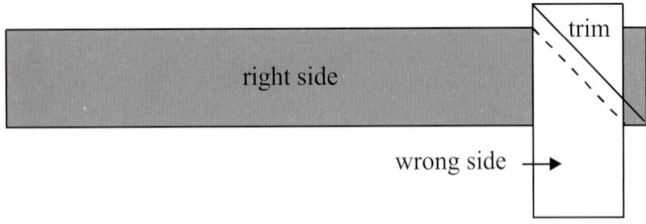

* Press the strip in half lengthwise, wrong sides together.

* Place the folded binding strip raw edges even with the raw edge of the quilt. Leave 8" free, and begin stitching the binding to the quilt a few inches beyond the center of one edge. Stitch with a 1/4" seam allowance; back tack to secure the seam.

* Miter binding at the corners. Stop stitching 1/4" from the edge and back tack. Fold the binding strip up, away from the quilt; it will fold nicely at a 45° angle. Fold it again to bring the strip edge along the raw edge of the quilt top. This fold should be even with the top edge of the quilt. Begin stitching at the fold, stitch through all layers.

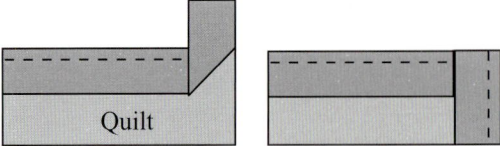

* Continue sewing around the quilt in this manner until you are within 12" of the starting point.

* To finish the binding, fold each strip back on itself so that the folds meet in the middle of the 12" gap. Finger press a crease at the folds. Trim the excess strip fabric 1" from both folds.

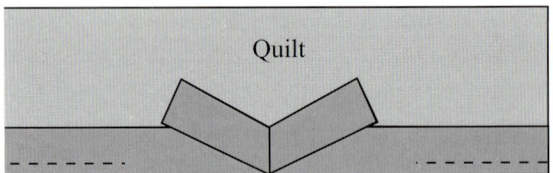

* Open the folded strips and place the strips right sides together as diagramed below. Fold the quilt out of your way to allow the binding strips to be aligned properly. Stitch the strips together with a diagonal seam. Trim the seam allowance to 1/4" and press the seam open.

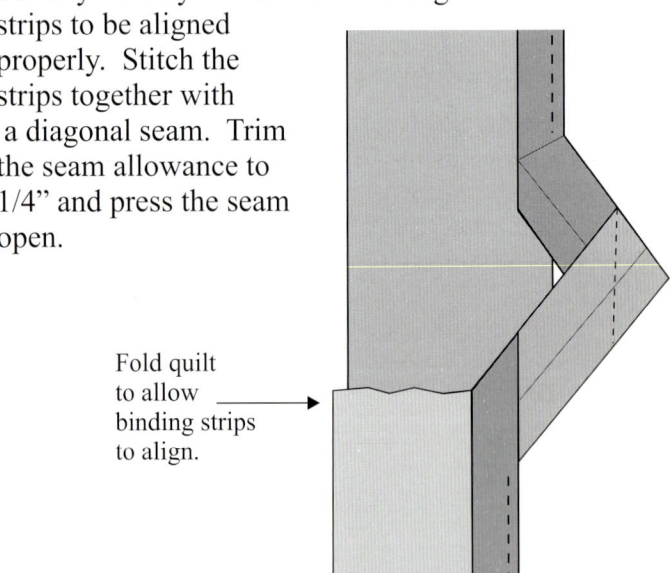

Fold quilt to allow binding strips to align.

* Fold the binding strip together again and finish stitching the binding strip to the edge of the project.

* Hand stitch the folded edge of the binding to the back side of the quilt with a blind stitch. Use a thread that matches the binding. The fold of the binding should just cover the seamline.

Piped Binding

This little technique is my latest favorite quilt-making shortcut. Shown to me by a quilting friend, this binding technique allows me to do a down n dirty, entirely machine sewn binding. It looks good, brings an extra dash of color to the outer edge of the quilt and is fast, fast, fast!

If you choose to use a piped binding, cut the number of binding strips listed in the instructions for your chosen quilt, cutting that number of binding strips and the same number of piping strips. (Spray starch will make your binding strips easier to handle.)

Cut two sets of strips:
  Piping - cut strips 1 ½" wide
  Binding - cut strips 1 1/8" wide

The resulting binding will be approximately ¼" wide plus a narrow pipe detail.

Stitch Piping strips together using diagonal seams, trim seams to ¼" and press open.

Stitch Binding strips together using diagonal seams, trim seams to ¼" and press open.

Sew the Piping and Binding strips together along the lengthwise edge using a ¼" seam. Press the seam toward the Binding strip.

Fold the strip in half and press.

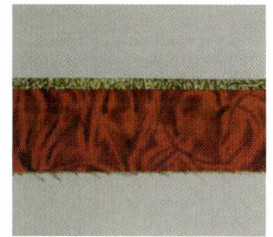

Place the **binding** fabric on the **backside** of quilt and sew in place using a ¼" seam.

Stitch binding to the quilt as detailed on page 4. When sewing the diagonal seam to join the ends, pay close attention to the intersection of the seam between the binding and piping strips to ensure a clean finish. Trim excess binding and press seam open.

Fold the Binding strip to the Front of the quilt. Using a thread to match the piping, top stitch in the ditch. A white thread has been used just to illustrate the stitching process. If you wish, a decorative thread or stitch can be used to secure the binding.

Before you commit to a large quilt, do a test run using scrap fabrics. You may wish to adjust the binding width by adding the same amount to each strip. Such as:
  Piping Strip: 1 5/8"
  Binding Strip: 1 ¼"

Triangulations™ Basics

The following directions are a quick introduction to the use of Triangulations™ grids. Please refer to the disc for more complete instructions.

Each gridded Triangulations™ square will yield 2 complete half square triangle units.

1. Open the correct page and print the number of triangle foundations necessary for your chosen quilt. Trim the Triangulations™ paper 1/8" from the outermost printed line.

2. Cut the fabric pieces slightly larger than the trimmed Triangulations™ paper, 1/4" larger is sufficient.

3. Place two fabric pieces right sides together. Position a Triangulations™ paper **on the wrong side of the light (background) fabric** and pin the paper to the fabric pair.

4. Stitch on all dotted lines. Follow the arrows for a continuous seam. Use a small stitch (18 - 20 stitches per inch) and a size 14 sewing machine needle to better perforate the paper.

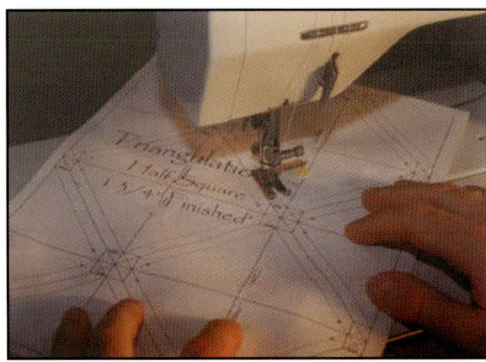

5. Cut on all solid lines using a rotary cutter and ruler. I generally trim off all excess from the edges first before I cut the unit into individual squares and then into triangles.

6. Snip off the points of the triangles on the "trim" line indicated to remove dog ears.

7. With the paper still attached, finger press the seam toward the dark fabric.

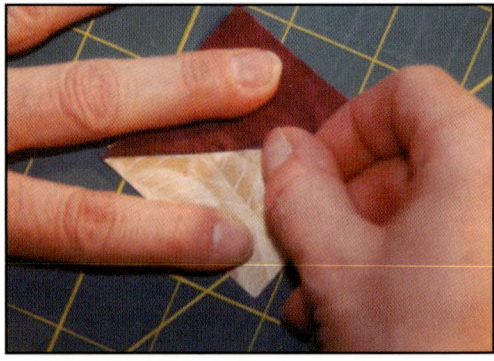

8. Remove the paper foundation. Pinch the center of the seam between the thumb and forefinger of you "wrong" hand. Pull the paper foundation from the square corner against your thumbnail.

Jacob's Ladder

Fabric Requirements and Cutting Instructions:

	Lap 59 ½" x 70" 20 - 10 ½" blocks	Double 80 ½" x 91" 42 - 10 ½" blocks
Background	3 yards	5 yards
A - rectangles 5" x 9 ¼"	31	64
C - 2 ¼" wide strips	7	14
E - 7 5/8" x 10" rectangles	11	15
First Border - 2 ¼" wide strips	6	8
Dark	4 ½ yards	7 ¼ yards
Final Border - Lengthwise grain strips - cut these first		
Sides	2 strips 4" x 67"	2 strips 4" x 87"
Top and Bottom	2 strips 4" x 64"	2 strips 4" x 84"
B - 5" x 9 ¼" rectangles	31	64
D - 2 ¼" wide strips	7	14
F - 7 5/8" x 10" rectangles	11	15
Binding - 2" wide strips	7	10
Backing	4 yards	5 ¾ yards

Alternate Cutting for traditional triangle method

Background
- **A** - 4 3/8" squares
  - cut once diagonally
- **E** - 4 ¾" squares
  - cut twice diagonally

A - 4 3/8" squares	62	128
- cut once diagonally	yield: 124 triangles	yield: 256 triangles
E - 4 ¾" squares	29	41
- cut twice diagonally	yield: 116 triangles	yield: 164 triangles

Dark
- **B** - 4 3/8" squares
  - cut once diagonally
- **F** - 4 ¾" squares
  - cut twice diagonally

B - 4 3/8" squares	62	128
- cut once diagonally	yield: 124 triangles	yield: 256 triangles
F - 4 ¾" squares	15	41
- cut twice diagonally	yield: 116 triangles	yield: 164 triangles

Block Construction

1. **Print Half Square Triangulations™ papers.
   Print page 34 - 3 ½" finished size.**

Print	Lap	31 copies
	Double	64 copies

2. **Print Quarter Square Triangulations™ papers.
   Print page 32 - 3 ½" finished size.**

Print	Lap	11 copies
	Double	15 copies

3. Construct half square triangles, place a 5" x 9 ¼" rectangle **A** of **Background Fabric** right sides together with rectangle **B** of **Dark Fabric**. Construct half square triangles following the Triangulations™ paper method. Each rectangle pair will yield four half square triangle units measuring 4" raw edge to raw edge. Repeat using all A and B rectangles.

Make

Lap	124
Double	256

4. Stitch 2 ¼" **C** and **D** strips together as diagramed below. Press the seam toward the **D** strips. Sub-cut the sewn strips into 2 ¼" units.

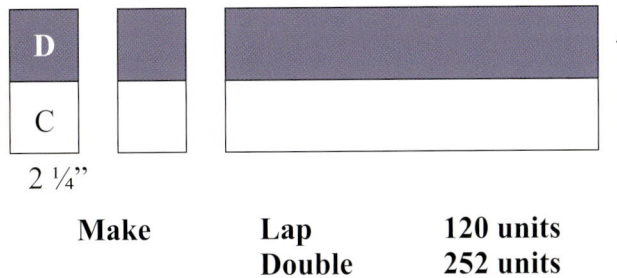

Make	Lap	120 units
	Double	252 units

5. Join units from step 4 above. Press seams to one side.

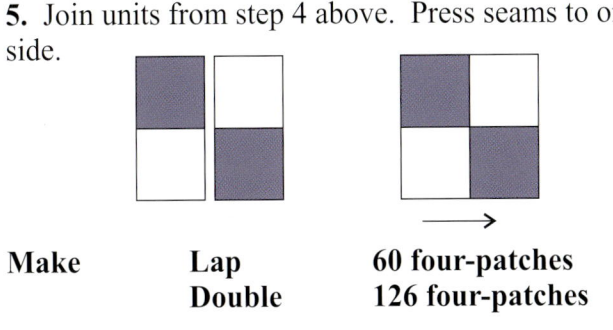

Make	Lap	60 four-patches
	Double	126 four-patches

6. Construct blocks as diagramed below. Press the seams as shown.

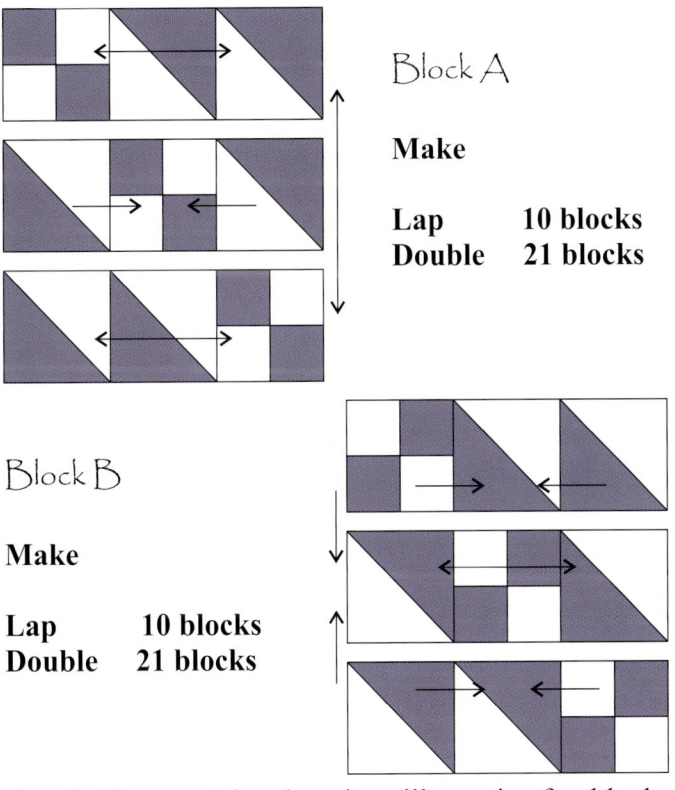

Block A

Make

Lap	10 blocks
Double	21 blocks

Block B

Make

Lap	10 blocks
Double	21 blocks

Four half square triangle units will remain after block construction. These units will be used as the corners of the pieced border strips.

7. Construct quarter square triangles using the 7 5/8" x 10" rectangles **E** of **Background Fabric** with the rectangles **F** of **Dark Fabric**. Each pair will yield eleven quarter square triangle units.

8. Stitch triangle pairs from step 7 together to create hour glass blocks.

9. Pull the last two or three stitches of the vertical seams that extend past the long seam into the ¼" seam allowance. This will allow you to split the long seam at the center; all of the seams will be rotating in the same direction and the bulk at the center will be distributed. The hour glass blocks measure 4" raw edge to raw edge.

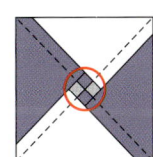

Make	Lap	58
	Twin	70
	Double	82

10. Join quarter square triangles and remaining half square triangles together. Seams can be pressed open to reduce bulk. Make 2 of each border strip.

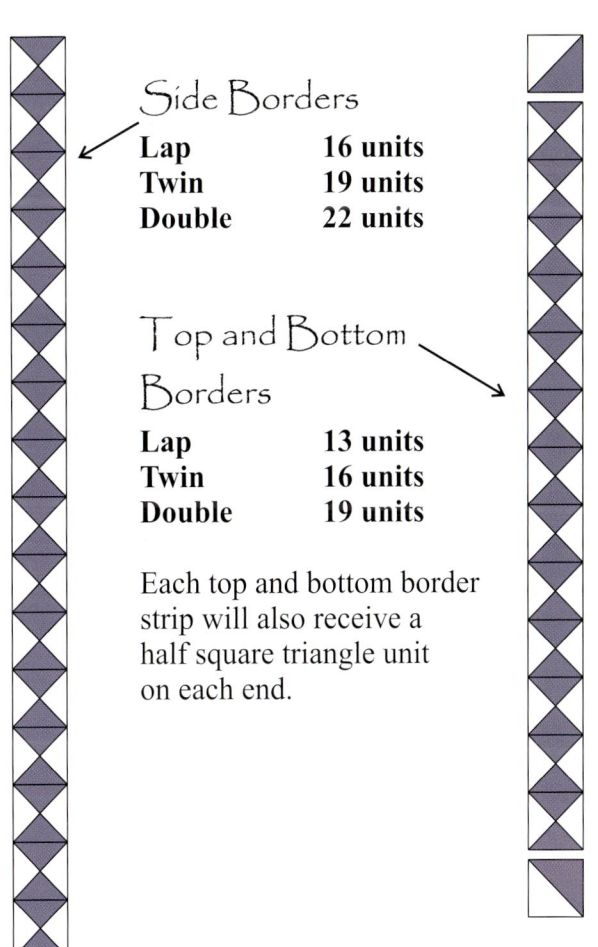

Side Borders

Lap	16 units
Twin	19 units
Double	22 units

Top and Bottom Borders

Lap	13 units
Twin	16 units
Double	19 units

Each top and bottom border strip will also receive a half square triangle unit on each end.

Quilt Top Assembly

1. Arrange and join blocks as diagramed below. Pay close attention to the placement of A and B blocks.

2. Diagonally piece the first border strips, and cut lengths as needed. Attach the side borders first and then the top and bottom borders. Press all seams toward the first border strips.

3. Attach the pieced border strips. Press seams toward the first border strips.

4. Trim the final borders strips to length as needed. Attach side borders first and then the top and bottom borders. Press all seams toward the final border strips.

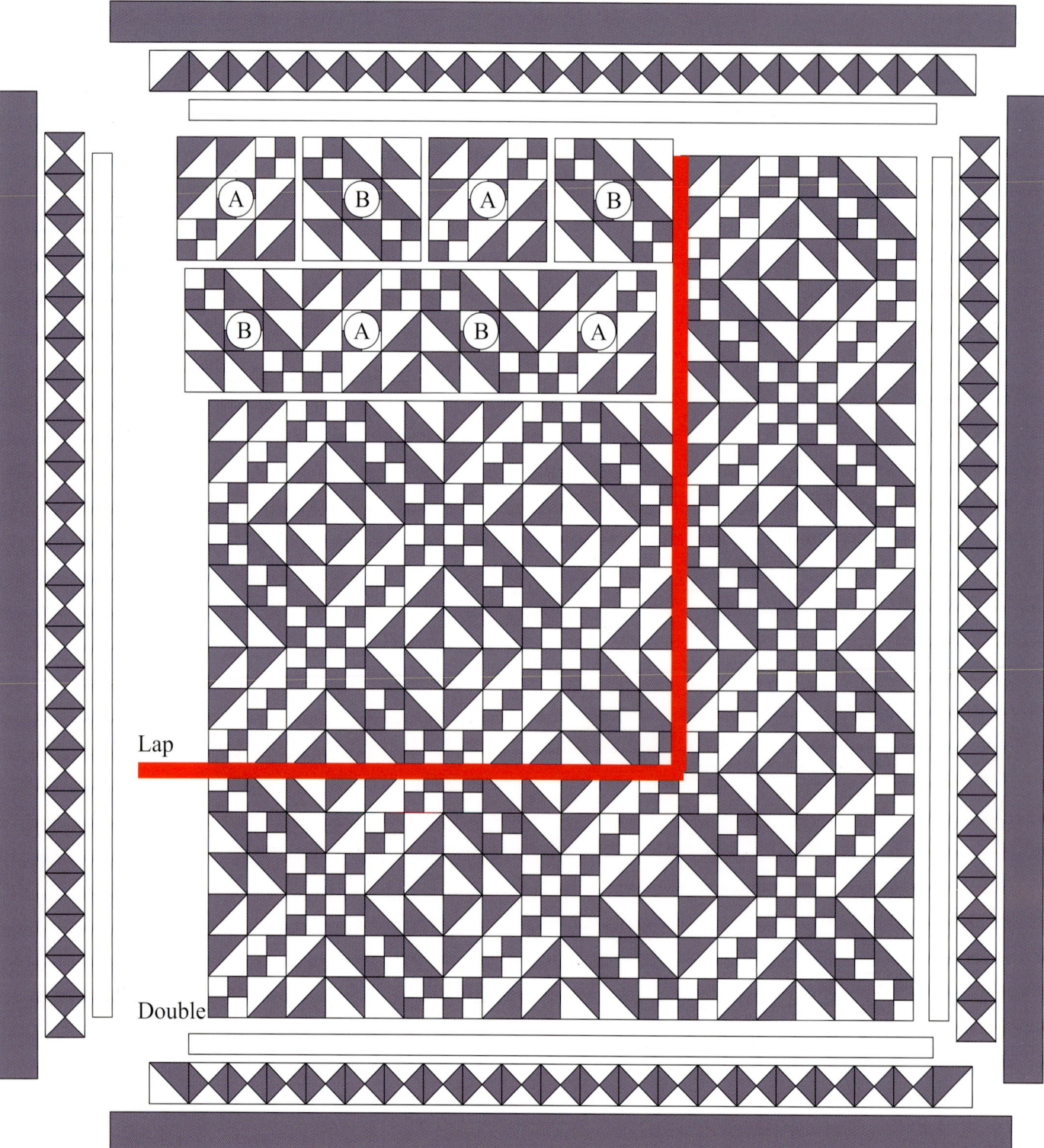

Double X

Fabric Requirements and Cutting Instructions:

	Lap 63 ½" x 76 ½" 49 - 9" blocks	Twin 76 ½" x 89" 71 - 9" blocks	Queen 89" x 102" 97 - 9" blocks
Assorted Light Fabrics	4 yards total	5 ¼ yards	6 ¾ yards
A - 6 ¾" x 10" rectangles	50	70	94
B - 2 ¾" squares	50	72	98
C - 5" squares	25	36	49
D - 4 ½" squares - cut twice diagonally	5	6	7
E - 7 5/8" squares - cut twice diagonally	3	3	4
Assorted Dark Fabrics	4 ½ yards total	5 ¾ yards	8 ¼ yards
F - 6 ¾" x 10" rectangles	50	70	94
G - 2 ¾" squares	48	70	96
H - 5" squares	24	35	48
I - 4 ½" squares - cut twice diagonally	6	7	8
J - 7 5/8" squares - cut twice diagonally	3	4	4
Binding - 2" wide strips	8	9	10
Backing	4 yards	5 ½ yards	7 ¼ yards

Alternate Cutting for traditional triangle method

Background
- **A** - 3 1/8" squares
  - cut once diagonally

| 300 | 420 | 560 |
| yield: 600 triangles | yield: 840 triangles | yield: 1120 triangles |

Dark
- **F** - 3 1/8" squares
  - cut once diagonally

| 300 | 420 | 560 |
| yield: 600 triangles | yield: 840 triangles | yield: 1120 triangles |

NOTE - Fabric Selection

I have a problem when selecting fabric...I cannot seem to stop. Why use 5 fabrics when 25 will do? This quilt was constructed using a wide palette of related fabrics; thus, the yardage given of light and dark fabrics is just a starting point, Multiple fat quarters can be used. Just have fun!

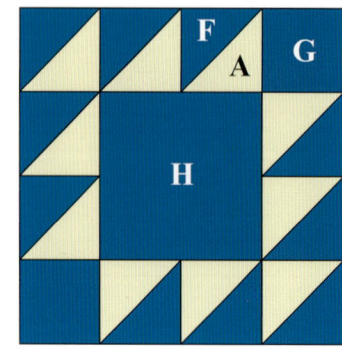

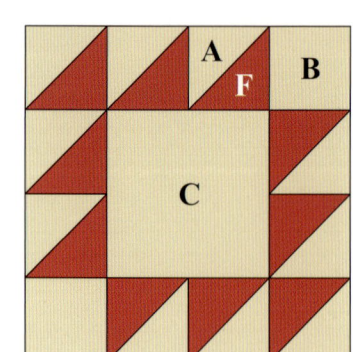

Block Construction

1. **Print Half Square Triangulations™ papers.
   Print page 24 - 2 ¼" finished size.**

Print		
	Lap	50 copies
	Twin	70 copies
	Queen	94 copies

2. Place a 6 ¾" x 10" rectangle **A** of **Light Fabric** right sides together with 6 ¾" x 10" rectangle **F** of **Dark Fabric**. Construct half square triangles following the Triangulations™ paper method. Each rectangle pair will yield twelve half square triangle units measuring 2 ¾" raw edge to raw edge. Repeat using all **A** and **F** rectangles.

Make	Lap	600
	Twin	840
	Queen	1120

3. Construct blocks as diagramed below. Pressing the seams as indicated by the arrows.

Make Dark Blocks
using half square triangle units with **Dark Fabric** squares **G** and **H**.

Make
Lap   24
Twin   35
Queen 48

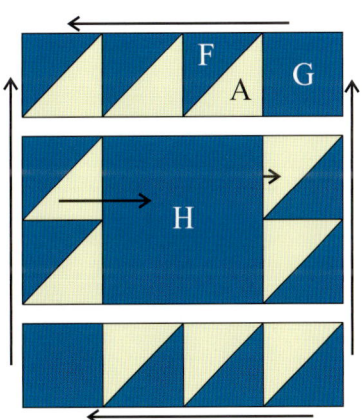

Make Light Blocks
using half square triangle units with **Light Fabric** squares **B** and **C**.

Make
Lap   25
Twin   36
Queen 49

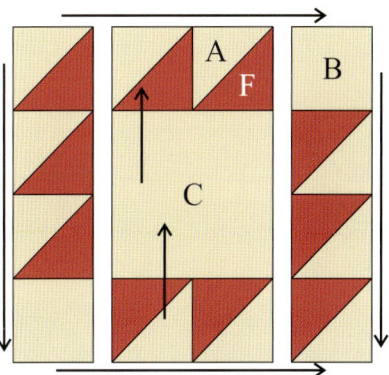

Make Dark Half Blocks
using half square triangle units with **Dark Fabric** triangles **I** and **J**.

Make
Lap   12
Twin   14
Queen 16

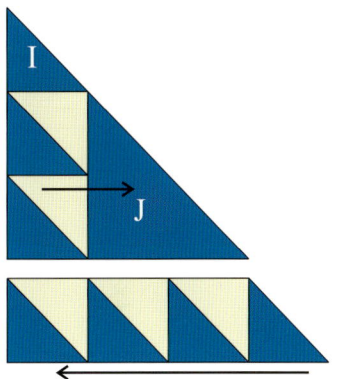

Make Light Half Blocks
using half square triangle units with **Light Fabric** triangles **D** and **E**.

Make
Lap   10
Twin   12
Queen 14

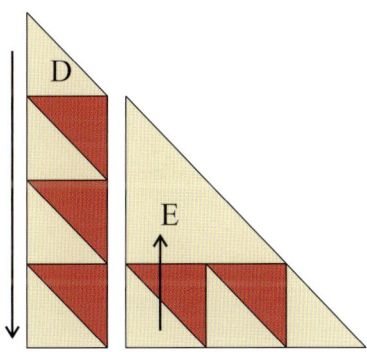

All quilts in this book are made using triangle foundation grids from the Triangulations™ 2.0 disc.

Other books that use Triangulations™ grids are available at your local quilt shop:

Table Runners ~ A Quilter's Dozen
Table Runners ~ A Second Helping
Mariner's Compass Quilts ~ Reach for the Stars

Quilt Top Assembly

1. Lay the quilt top out on a floor or design wall paying careful attention to the position of the light and dark blocks. The blocks will be assembled in diagonal rows.

2. Join blocks and half blocks together into rows. Press all seams toward the dark blocks and dark half blocks. Stitch the assembled rows together. Press all seams in one direction.

Lap

Twin

Queen

Christmas Cactus

Fabric Requirements and Cutting Instructions:

	Lap 51" x 63 ½" 32 - 9" blocks	Twin 76 ½" x 89" 72 - 9" blocks
Assorted Light Tan Fabrics	2 ¼ yards total	4 yards
A - 7 5/8" x 10" rectangles	28	56
B - 2" squares	72	156
C - 3 3/8" squares – cut twice diagonally ⊠	4	6
Assorted Green Fabrics	2 ¾ yards	5 ½ yards
D - 7 5/8" x 10" rectangles	14	28
E - 6 7/8" squares – cut once diagonally ◺	16	36
F - 2" squares	35	77
G - 5 1/8" squares – cut once diagonally ◺	5	7
H - 9 ¾" square – cut twice diagonally ⊠	1	2
I - 3 3/8" squares – cut twice diagonally ⊠	3	4
Binding - 2" wide strips	6	9
Assorted Red Fabrics	2 ¼ yards	5 yards
J - 7 5/8" x 10" rectangles	14	28
K - 6 7/8" squares – cut once diagonally ◺	16	36
L - 2" squares	35	77
M - 5 1/8" squares – cut once diagonally ◺	5	7
N - 9 ¾" square – cut twice diagonally ⊠	1	2
O - 3 3/8" squares – cut twice diagonally ⊠	3	4
Backing	3 ½ yards	5 ¾ yards

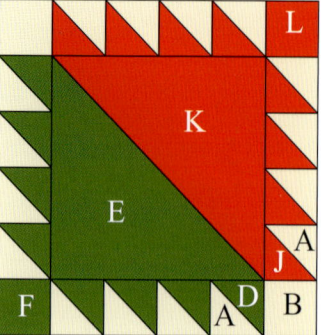

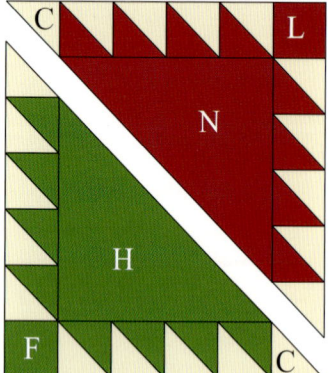

Alternate Cutting for traditional triangle method

Assorted Light Tan Fabrics
   A - 2 3/8" squares
      - cut once diagonally ◺   320   672
      yield: 640 triangles   yield: 1344 triangles

Assorted Green Fabrics
   D - 2 3/8" squares
      - cut once diagonally ◺   160   336
      yield: 320 triangles   yield: 672 triangles

Assorted Red Fabrics
   J - 2 3/8" squares
      - cut once diagonally ◺   160   336
      yield: 320 triangles   yield: 672 triangles

Block Construction

1. Print Half Square Triangulations™ papers.
Print page 18 - 1 ½" finished size.

Print		
	Lap	28 copies
	Twin	56 copies

2. Place a 7 5/8" x 10" rectangle **A** of **Light Tan Fabric** right sides together with 7 5/8" x 10" rectangle **D** of **Green Fabric**. Construct half square triangles following the Triangulations™ paper method. Each rectangle pair will yield 24 half square triangle units measuring 2" raw edge to raw edge. Repeat using all **A** and **D** rectangles. Repeat using remaining **A** rectangles of **Light Tan Fabric** with **J** rectangles of **Red Fabric**.

Make	Green/Tan	Red/Tan
Lap	320	320
Twin	672	672

3. Construct blocks as diagramed below. Pressing the seams as indicated by the arrows.

Make Blocks using half square triangle units from step 2 above with **Red and Green Fabric** triangles **K** and **E**, squares **L** and **F** and **Tan Fabric** squares **B**.

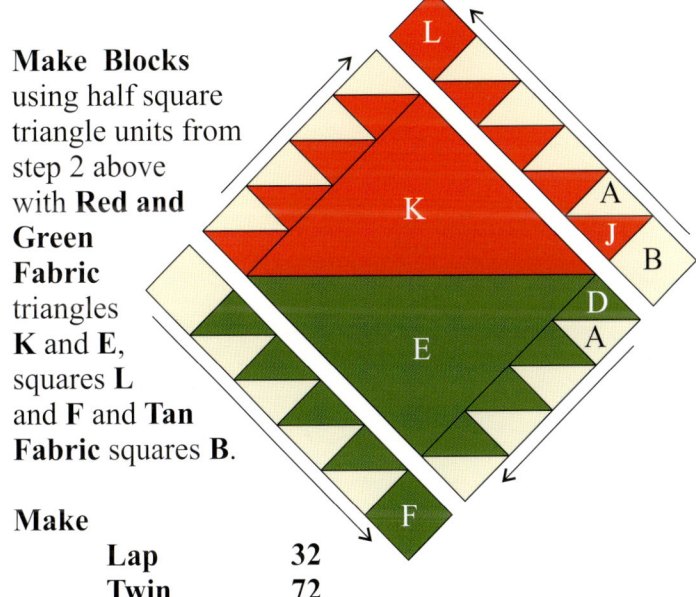

Make		
Lap	32	
Twin	72	

Make Green and **Red** half blocks to be used at the top and bottom of the quilt top.

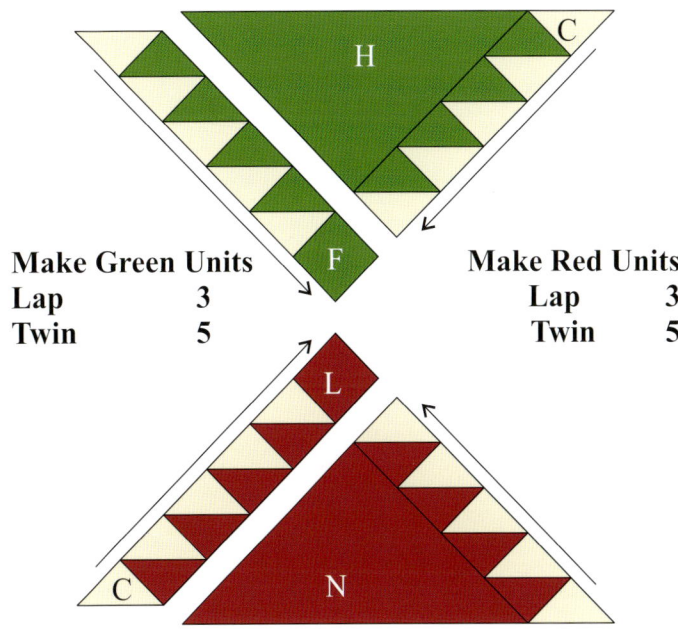

Make Green Units		Make Red Units	
Lap	3	Lap	3
Twin	5	Twin	5

Make Left and **Right** half blocks to be used at the sides of the quilt top.

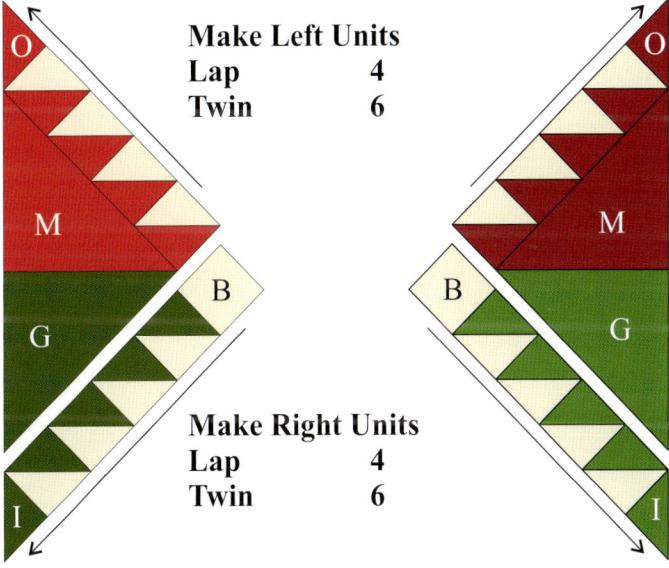

Make Left Units	
Lap	4
Twin	6

Make Right Units	
Lap	4
Twin	6

Make 2 Green and **2 Red** quarter/corner blocks.

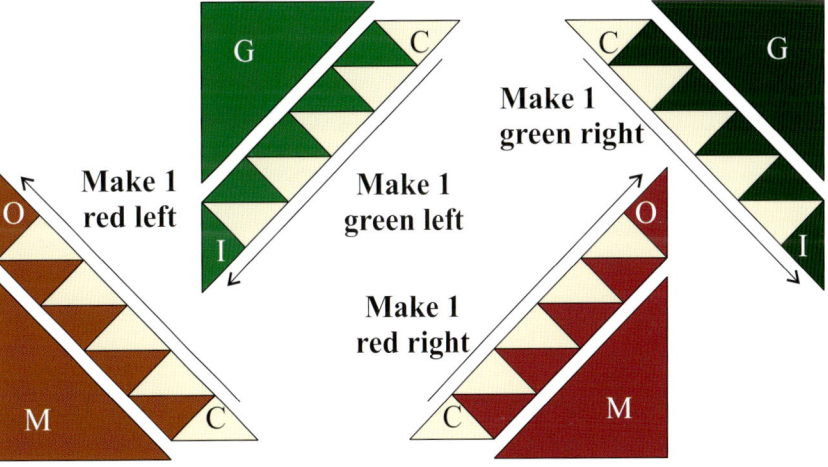

Make 1 red left
Make 1 green left
Make 1 green right
Make 1 red right

Quilt Top Assembly

1. Lay the quilt top out on a floor or design wall Arrange the blocks as diagramed with red at the top of each block. The blocks will be assembled in diagonal rows.

2. Join blocks and half blocks together into rows. Press all seams open to reduce bulk.

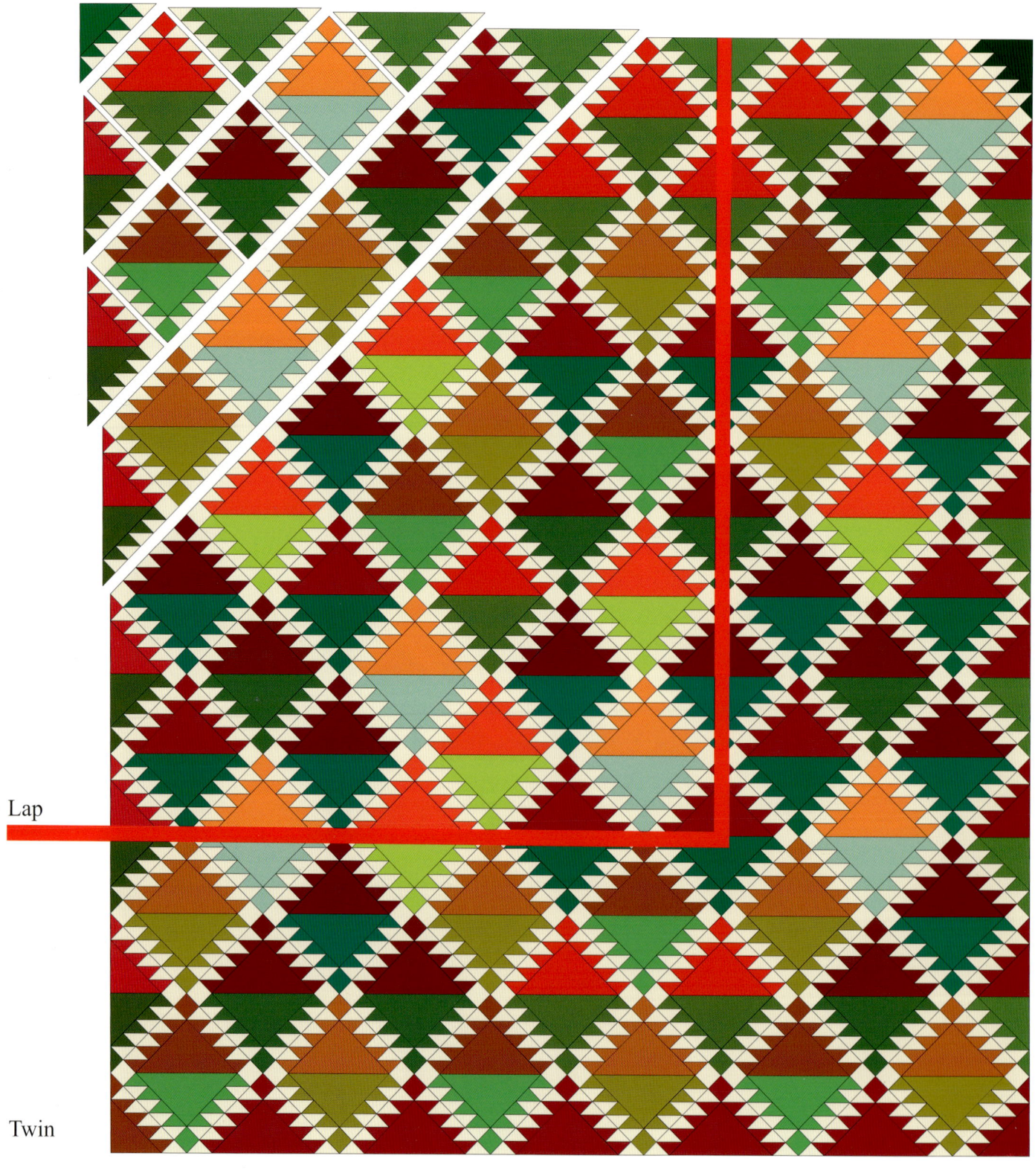

Lap

Twin

Feathered Streak of Lightening

Fabric Requirements and Cutting Instructions:

	Twin 78" x 86"	Queen 98" x 106"
Light Tan Fabric	1 ½ yards total	2 ¼ yards
A - 8 ½ " squares	20	32
B - 3 ¾" squares - cut twice diagonally	28	40
Assorted Navy Fabrics	1 ¼ yards	2 yards
C - 8 ½" squares	20	32
Medium Tan	1 yard	1 ¾ yards
D - 5" x 9 ¼" rectangles	6	9
E - 4" squares	48	80
F - 3 3/8" squares - cut once diagonally	3	4
Red	1 ¼ yard	1 ¾ yards
G - 5" x 9 ¼" rectangles	6	9
H - 6 ¼" squares - cut each 6 ¼" square twice diagonally	18	29
I - 3 3/8" squares - cut once diagonally	6	8
Blue Background, Border and Binding	5 ½ yards	8 ½ yards
J - Borders - lengthwise grain	6 strips 4" x 92"	6 strips 4" x 102"
K - 21" squares - cut twice diagonally	6	9
L - 10 ¾ squares - cut once diagonally	3	4
M - 6 ¼" squares - cut twice diagonally	8	10
N - 3 3/8" squares - cut once diagonally	2	2
Binding 2" strips	9	11
Backing	5 ½ yards	9 yards

Alternate Cutting for traditional triangle method

Light Tan Fabric		
A - 2 5/8" squares - cut once diagonally	174 yield: 348 triangles	282 yield: 564 triangles
Navy		
C - 2 5/8" squares - cut once diagonally	174 yield: 348 triangles	282 yield: 564 triangles
Medium Tan		
D - 4 3/8" squares - cut once diagonally	11 yield: 22 triangles	18 yield: 36 triangles
Red		
G - 4 3/8" squares - cut once diagonally	11 yield: 22 triangles	18 yield: 36 triangles

Block Construction

1. **Print Half Square Triangulations™ papers. Print page 20 - 1 ¾" finished size.**

Print	Twin	20 copies
	Queen	32 copies

2. **Print Half Square Triangulations™ papers. Print page 34 - 3 ½" finished size**

Print	Twin	6 copies
	Queen	9 copies

3. Place an 8 ½" square **A** of **Light Tan Fabric** right sides together with an 8 ½" square **C** of **Navy Fabric**. Construct half square triangles following the Triangulations™ paper method. Each rectangle pair will yield eighteen half square triangle units measuring 2 ¼" raw edge to raw edge. Repeat using all **A** and **C** squares.

4. Construct half square triangles using 5" x 9 ¼" rectangle **G** of **Red Fabric** right sides together with 5" x 9 ¼" rectangle **D** of **Medium Tan Fabric**. Each rectangle pair will yield four half square triangle units measuring 4" raw edge to raw edge. Repeat using all **D** and **G** rectangles.

5. Construct feathered units as diagramed at the right. Pressing the seams as indicated by the arrows. Trim the excess half square triangle unit that extends beyond the edge of the smaller feathered units.

6. Construct border units as diagramed below. Pressing the seams as indicated by the arrows.

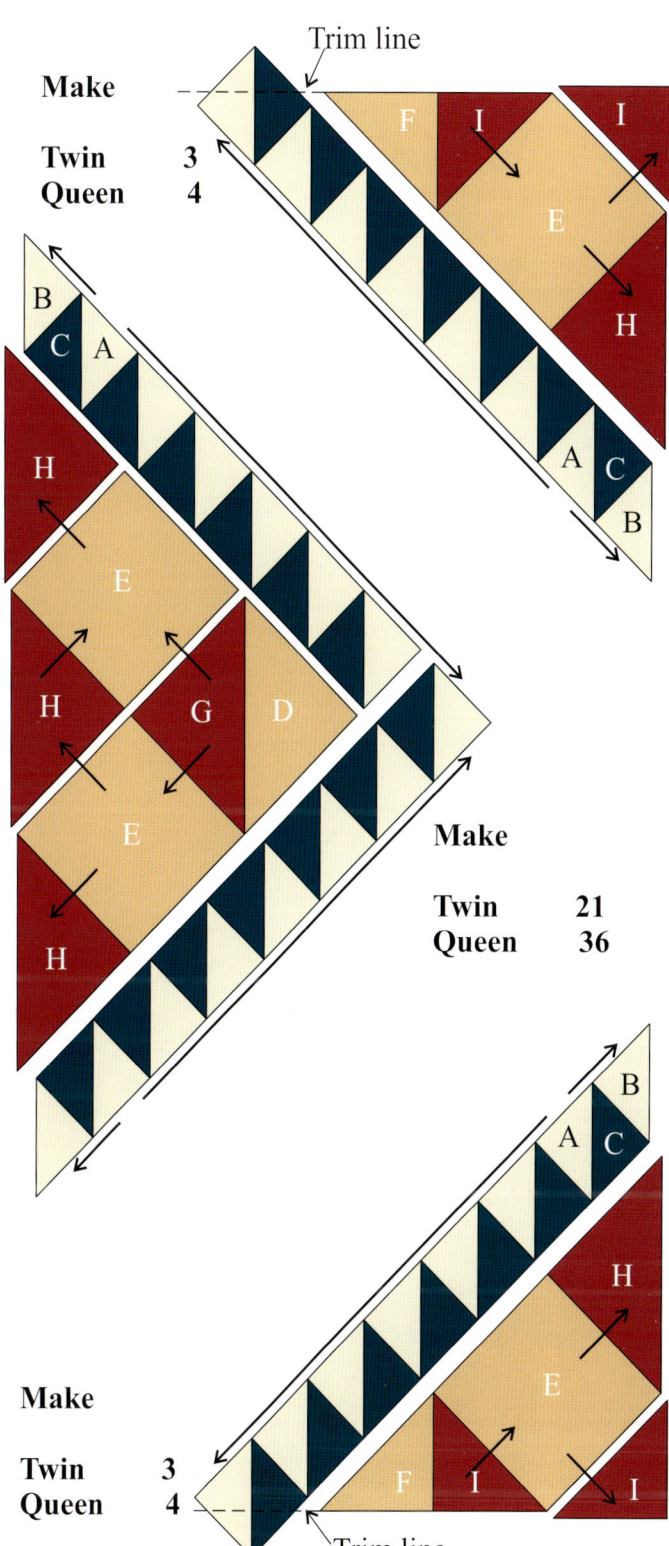

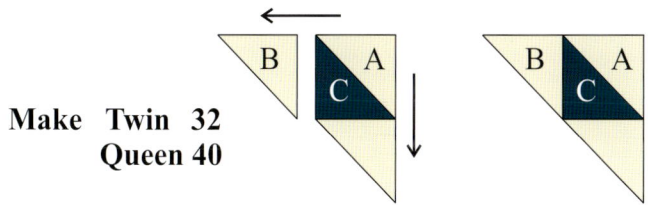

Make Twin 32
      Queen 40

7. Join border units together as diagramed below using Blue N and M pieces. Construct 2 border strips.

Each twin strip will be constructed using 16 units from step 6. Each queen strip will be constructed using 20 units from step 6.

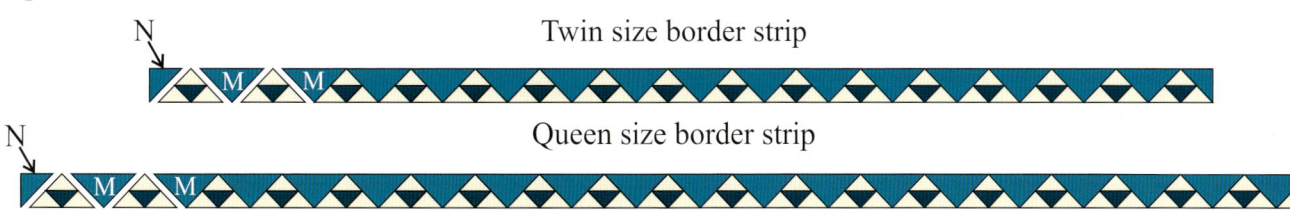

Twin size border strip

Queen size border strip

Quilt Top Assembly

1. Layout the quilt top in vertical rows as diagramed below.

2. Join the pieced triangles in rows. Attach the rows together, cutting the lengthwise grain border strips to size as needed. Press the seams toward unpieced strips where able. Press all other long seams open.

3. Trim the border strips to length for the top and bottom border and attach. Press the seam toward the top and bottom border strips.

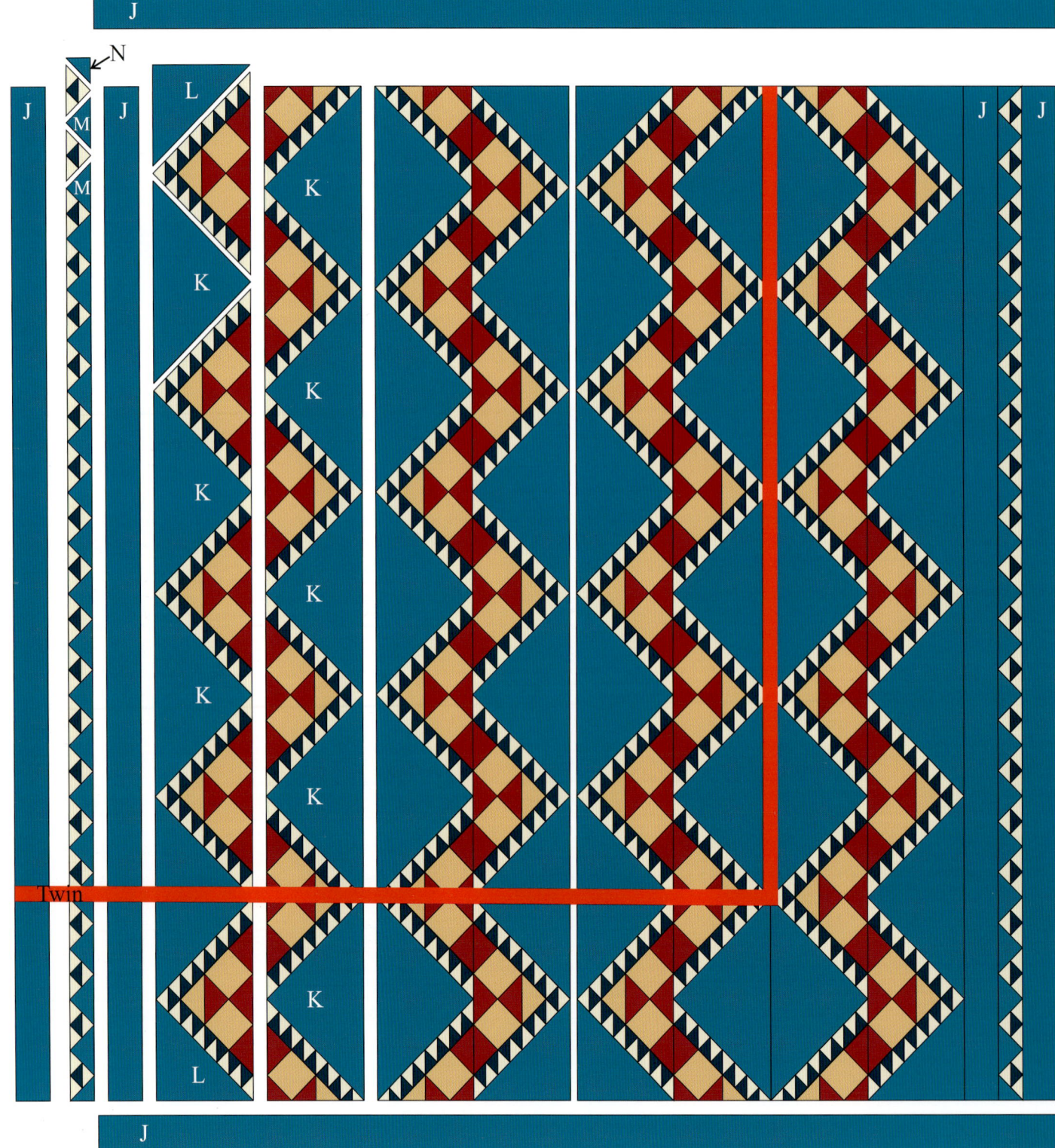

Sawtooth Diamond

Sawtooth Diamond
Finished Size: 80½" x 80½"

Fabric Requirements and Cutting Instructions

Background - Light Blue   5 yards
- A - 23 squares 8 ½"
- B - 1 square 7 ½"
- C - 2 squares 15 3/8" cut once diagonally
- D - 2 squares 36 ¼" cut once diagonally
- E - Final Border - 4 strips 4" x 84" - cut first!

Dark Blue   3 ¾ yards
- F - 23 squares 8 ½"
- G - 2 squares 9 ¼" cut once diagonally
- H - 2 squares 24 1/8" cut once diagonally
- Binding - 9 strips 2"

Backing 86" x 86"   5 yards

Alternate Cutting for traditional triangle method
Light Blue Fabric
  A - 200 squares 2 5/8"
       - cut once diagonally   yield: 400 triangles
Dark Blue
  F - 200 squares 2 5/8"
       - cut once diagonally   yield: 400 triangles

Block Construction

1. Print Half Square Triangulations™ papers. Print 23 copies of page 20 - 1 ¾" finished size.

2. Place an 8 ½" square **A** of **Light Blue Fabric** right sides together with an 8 ½" square **F** of **Dark Blue Fabric**. Construct half square triangles following the Triangulations™ paper method. Each rectangle pair will yield eighteen half square triangle units measuring 2 ¼" raw edge to raw edge. Repeat using all **A** and **F** squares.

3. Join half square triangle units together as diagramed. Press seams open or in one direction. **Make 2 of each strip diagramed below and at right.**

Round 1
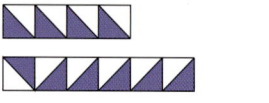
Make 2
4 units
6 units

Round 2
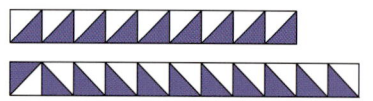
Make 2
9 units
11 units

Round 3
Make 2
18 units
16 units

Round 4
Make 2
28 units
26 units

Round 5
Make 2
42 units
40 units

Quilt Top Assembly

1. Stitch **Round 1** half square strips to the sides of **Light Blue** square **B**. Press seams toward **B**.

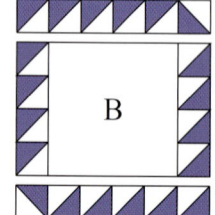
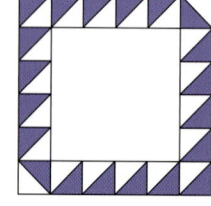

2. Attach **Dark Blue** triangles **G** to each side of the square from step 1 above. Press seams toward triangles G.

NOTE: All triangles (C, D, G and H) appear slightly oversized. Fold the triangle to find the center and match to the center of the pieced unit. The edges will align and the pieced unit will float. This allows the next round of half square triangles to be the mathematically correct length.

3. Continue adding triangles and pieced strips. Pressing all seams toward large triangles.

4. Trim final border strips to length as needed. Attach side borders first and then the top and bottom borders. Press all seams toward the final border strips.

Pine Trees

Pine Trees

Finished Size: 54" x 54"

Four - 18" blocks

Fabric Requirements and Cutting Instructions:

Background   3 ¼ yards
- A - 26 rectangles 6 ¾" x 10"
- B - 20 squares 2 ¾"
- C - 9 squares 5"
- D - 8 rectangles 2 ¾" x 18 ½"
- E - 8 squares 6 ⅞" cut twice diagonally
- Binding - 6 strips 2" wide

Assorted Dark Fabrics   2 ½ yards
- F - 26 rectangles 6 ¾" x 10"
- G - 8 squares 7 ⅝" cut once diagonally
- H - trunk - 16 rectangles 2 ⅛" x 5 ⅜"

Backing 60" x 60"   3 ½ yards

---

*Alternate Cutting for traditional triangle method"

Background
- A - 156 squares 3 ⅛"
  - cut once diagonally   yield: 312 triangles

Dark Purple
- D - 156 squares 3 ⅛"
  - cut once diagonally   yield: 312 triangles

Fabric Selection Note

This quilt was constructed using a fat quarter packet of 15 fabrics. I cut extra 6 ¾" x 10" rectangles of each of the 15 hand dyed fabrics and background fabric when constructing my half square triangles. While this did cost a little extra fabric and time, it allowed me the full range of colors when placing the triangles in the quilt construction.

Block Construction

1. **Print Half Square Triangulations™ papers. Print 26 copies of page 24 - 2 ¼" finished size.**

2. **Half Square Triangle Units**
Construct 2 ¼" half square triangles using the 6 ¾" x 10" rectangles **A** of **Background Fabric** with the 6 ¾" x 10" rectangles **F** of **Dark Fabric.**

Each rectangle pair will yield twelve half square triangle units, measuring 2 ¾" raw edge to raw edge. Press the seam toward the dark fabric.

3. Stitch a quarter square triangle **E** of **Background Fabric** to each side of the **Tree Trunk** strips **H**. Align the square corners of the background triangles as shown below. Press the seams as indicated by the arrows. Trim the end of the trunk strip to complete the trunk unit. **Make 16.**

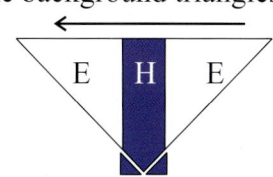

4. Join trunk units from step 3 to **Dark Fabric** triangles **G**. Press the seam open. **Make 16.**

5. Join trunk units from step 4 together. Press seams open. Add half square triangle units and Background Fabric squares B to the sides to complete the blocks. Press all seams open to reduce bulk.

       Make 4 Pine Tree blocks.

6. Construct sashing strips and border units using the remaining half square triangle units. Press all seams open to reduce bulk.

Sash Strips
Make 12

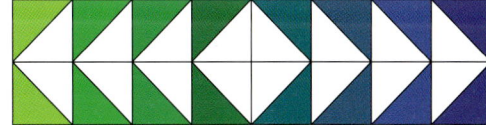

Border Units   **Make 12**

Quilt Top Assembly

Join the pieced blocks together with the sashing strips, border units and remaining background fabric pieces. Press all seams open.

Ocean Waves

Ocean Waves

Finished Size: 35 ½" x 49 ½"
Seven - 10 ½" blocks

Fabric Requirements and Cutting Instructions

Background   2 ½ yards
- A - 21 squares 8 ½"
- B - 8 squares 4"
- C - 17 squares 4 3/8" cut once diagonally
- D - 24 squares 2 5/8" cut once diagonally
- E - 18 squares 2 ¼"
- F - 5 squares 6 ¼" cut twice diagonally

Assorted Dark Fabrics   2 yards
- G - 21 squares 8 ½"
- H - 14 squares 2 ¼"
- I - 24 squares 2 5/8" cut once diagonally
- Binding - 4 strips 2"

Backing 40" x 55"   1 ¾ yards

Alternate Cutting for traditional triangle method

Background
    A - 187 squares 2 5/8"
        - cut once diagonally   yield: 374 triangles

Assorted Dark Fabrics
    G - 187 squares 2 5/8"
        - cut once diagonally   yield: 374 triangles

Block Construction

1. **Print Half Square Triangulations™ papers. Print 21 copies of page 20 - 1 ¾" finished size.**

2. Place an 8 ½" square **A** of **Light Blue Fabric** right sides together with an 8 ½" square **G** of **Dark Blue Fabric**. Construct half square triangles following the Triangulations™ paper method. Each rectangle pair will yield eighteen half square triangle units measuring 2 ¼" raw edge to raw edge. Repeat using all **A** and **G** squares.

3. Construct blocks as diagramed below. Pressing all seams open to reduce bulk.

Block A
Make 1 Center Block
using half square triangle units with **Background Fabric** squares and triangles **B**, **C** and **D**, and **Dark Fabric** squares **H**.

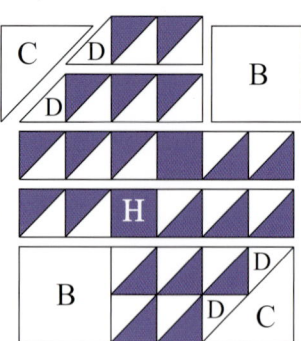

Block B
Make 6 Blocks
using half square triangle units with **Background Fabric** squares and triangles **B, C, D** and **E**, and **Dark Fabric** squares **H**.

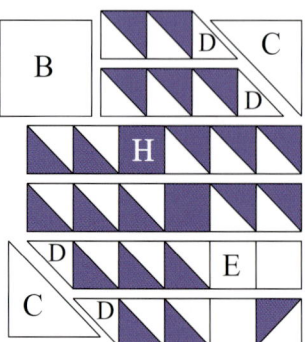

Block C
Make 10 Small Blocks
using half square triangle units with **Background Fabric** triangles **C** and **D**, and **Dark Fabric** triangles **I**.

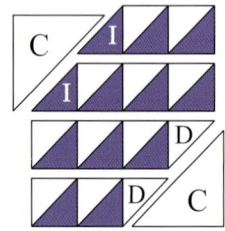

Block D
Make 8 Right Side Blocks
using half square triangle units with **Background Fabric** triangles **F**, and **Dark Fabric** triangles **I**.

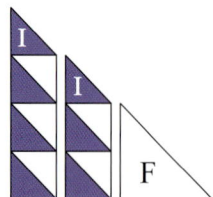

Block E
Make 6 Left Side Blocks
using half square triangle units with **Background Fabric** triangles **F**, and **Dark Fabric** triangles **I**.

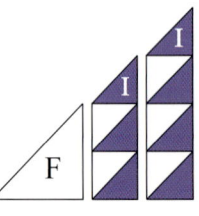

Block F
Make 4 Left Side Blocks using half square triangle units with **Background Fabric** triangles **F**.

Block G
Make 2 Right Side Blocks using half square triangle units with **Background Fabric** triangles **F**.

Quilt Top Assembly

Arrange the blocks in diagonal rows. Pay close attention to the placement of the light and dark triangles within the blocks as you position them.

Starry Path

Fabric Requirements and Cutting Instructions:

	Twin 64 1/4" x 84" 48 – 9 7/8" blocks	Queen 84" x 84" 64 – 9 7/8" blocks
Light Tan Background	5 yards	6 yards
A - 8 ½" squares	32	43
B - 3 ¾ squares — cut twice diagonally	24	40
C - 8 ¾" squares — cut twice diagonally	31	32
D - 3" x 8" rectangles	14	16
E - 3 3/8" squares — cut once diagonally	9	10
Assorted Burgundy Prints	5 ½ yards	6 ½ yards
F - 8 ½" squares	32	43
G - 3 ¾ squares — cut twice diagonally	24	40
H - 8 ¾" squares — cut twice diagonally	31	32
I - 3" x 8" rectangles	14	16
J - 3 3/8" squares — cut once diagonally	9	10
Binding - 2" wide strips	8	9
Backing	5 yards	7 ½ yards

Alternate Cutting for traditional triangle method

Light Tan Background		
A - 2 5/8" squares — cut once diagonally	288 yield: 576 triangles	384 yield: 768 triangles
Assorted Burgundy Prints		
F - 2 5/8" squares — cut once diagonally	288 yield: 576 triangles	384 yield: 768 triangles

Block Construction

1. **Print Half Square Triangulations™ papers. Print page 20 - 1 ¾" finished size.**

Print	Twin	32 copies
	Queen	43 copies

2. Place an 8 ½" square **A** of **Light Tan Background** right sides together with an 8 ½" square **F** of

Burgundy Fabric. Construct half square triangles following the Triangulations™ paper method. Each rectangle pair will yield eighteen half square triangle units measuring 2 ¼" raw edge to raw edge. Repeat using all **A** and **F** squares.

Make	Twin	576
	Queen	768

3. Stitch pairs of half square triangle units together as shown. Press the seam as indicated by the arrow.

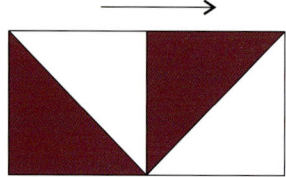

Make Twin 288
Queen 384

4. Join pairs together to create pinwheel units. After checking that the points match, pull the two or three stitches of the vertical seam that extend past the long seam into the 1/4" seam allowance. This will allow the final seam to be swirled and pressed so that all of the seams are rotating in the same direction, distributing the bulk in the center of the unit.

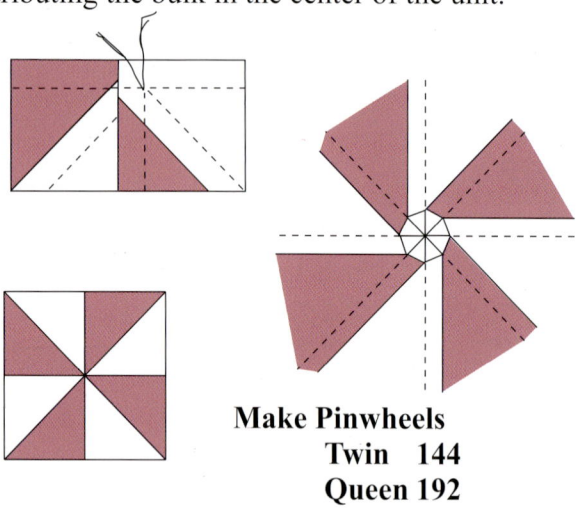

Make Pinwheels
Twin 144
Queen 192

5. Join sets of 3 pinwheel units together as diagramed below. Press seams open or in one direction.

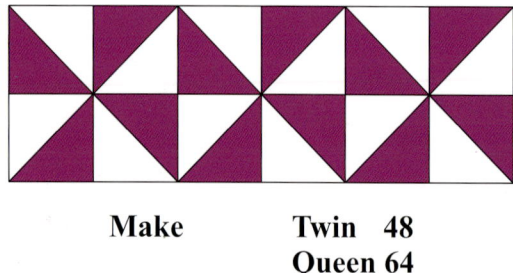

Make Twin 48
Queen 64

6. Stitch **C** and **H** triangles together as shown. Press the seam toward the **C** triangle.

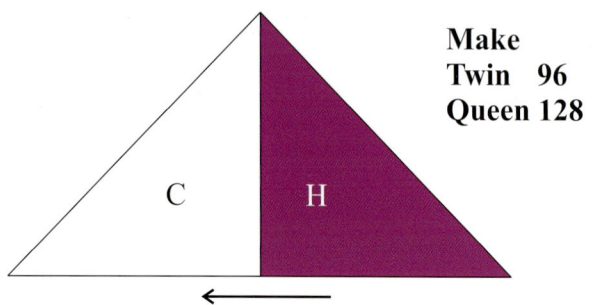

Make
Twin 96
Queen 128

7. Stitch **G** and **B** triangles together as shown. Press the seam toward the **G** triangle.

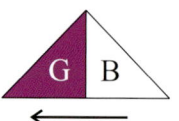

Make
Twin 96
Queen 128

8. Construct blocks as diagramed below. Pressing the seams as indicated by the arrows. Completed block will measure 10 3/8" square when measure from raw edge to raw edge.

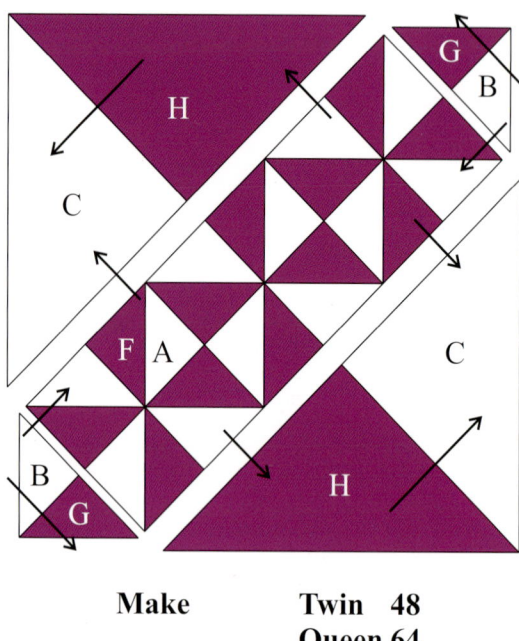

Make Twin 48
Queen 64

Pieced Border Construction

1. Press as indicated by the arrows.

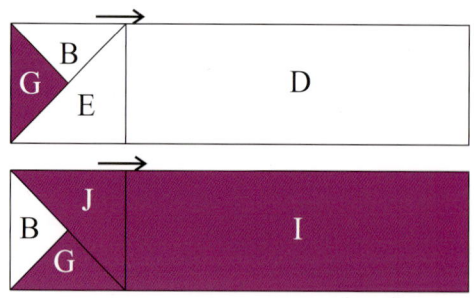

Make Twin 14 of each border unit
Queen 16 of each border unit

2. Stitch the remaining **Light Tan Background E** and **Burgundy Fabric J** 3 3/8" half square triangles together as diagramed at the right. Press the seam toward the Burgundy triangle. **Make 4** corner units.

Quilt Top Assembly

1. Assemble the blocks and pieced border units into rows. Sew the rows together to form the quilt top: twin - 6 x 8; and queen - 8 x 8. Notice that all of the numbers are even numbers. This ensures that the secondary pattern created as the blocks intersect will be a completed pattern.

2. If an optional final border is desired, cut the final borders to fit and apply to the quilt top, attach the side borders first and then the top and bottom borders. Press all seams toward the border strips.

35

Kansas Troubles Baby Quilt

Kansas Troubles Baby Quilt

Finished Size: 44 ¼" x 61 ¼"

Six - 12" blocks

Fabric Requirements and Cutting Instructions:

Background Fabric   3 ¾ yards
- **A** - 4 rectangles 7 ¾" x 10" - block construction
- **B** - 7 rectangles 6 ½" x 9 ½" - pieced border units
- **C** - 24 squares 2"
- **D** - 12 squares 6 7/8" - cut once diagonally
- **E** - 2 squares 12 ½"
- **F** - 2 squares 9 3/8" - cut once diagonally
- **G** - 2 squares 18 ¼" - cut twice diagonally

Final Borders - Lengthwise grain strips - cut first!
- **H** - Side Border - 2 strips 3 ½" x 55 ¾" -
- **I** - Top and Bottom - 2 strips 3 ½" x 44 ¾"

Binding - 4 strips 2" wide

Dark Fabric   1 ½ yard
- **J** - 4 rectangles 7 ¾" x 10" - block construction
- **K** - 7 rectangles 6 ½" x 9 ½" - pieced border units
- **L** - 12 squares 3 7/8" - cut once diagonally
- **M** - 12 squares 2 3/8" - cut once diagonally

Backing 50" x 66"

Alternate Cutting for traditional triangle method

Background Fabric
- **A** - 48 squares 2 3/8"
  - cut once diagonally   yield: 96 triangles
- **B** - 42 squares 3"
  - cut once diagonally   yield: 84 triangles

Dark Fabric
- **J** - 48 squares 2 3/8"
  - cut once diagonally   yield: 96 triangles
- **K** - 42 squares 3"
  - cut once diagonally   yield: 84 triangles

Block Construction

1. Print Half Square Triangulations™ papers. Print 4 copies of page 18 - 1 ½" finished size.

2. Construct 2" half square triangles using the 7 ¾" x 10" rectangles **A** of **Background Fabric** with the 7 ¾" x 10" rectangles **J** of **Dark Fabric**. Each rectangle pair will yield 24 half square triangle units measuring 2" raw edge to raw edge. **Make 96 half square triangle units**. These triangle units will be used in the block construction.

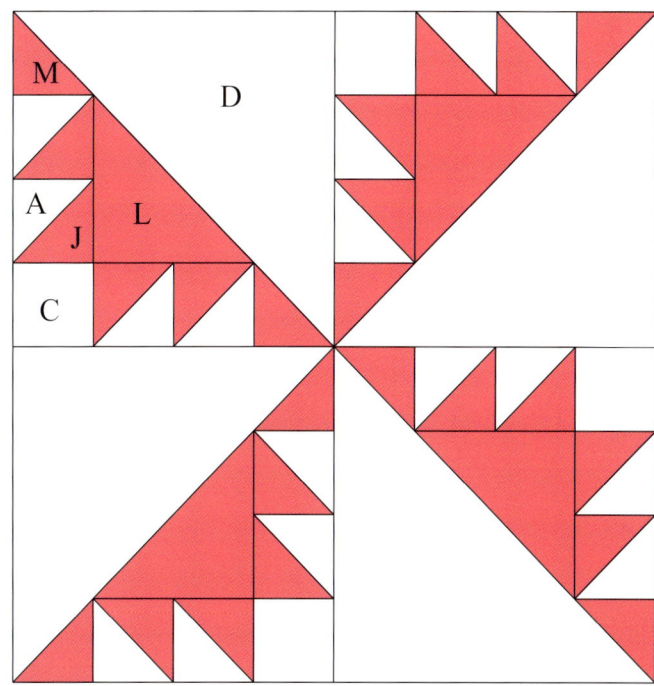

3. Make 24 Quarter Blocks using half square triangle units from step 2 with **Background Fabric** triangles **D** and squares **C**, and **Dark Fabric** triangles **L** and **M**. Press the seams as indicated by the arrows. Unit will measure 6 ½" square.

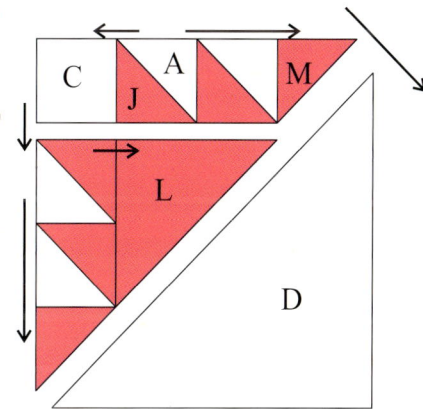

4. Join quarter block units together as diagramed below. After checking that the points match, pull the two or three stitches of the vertical seam that extend past the long seam into the ¼" seam allowance. This will allow the final seam to be swirled and pressed so that all of the seams are rotating in the same direction, distributing the bulk in the center of the block. Block will measure 12 ½".

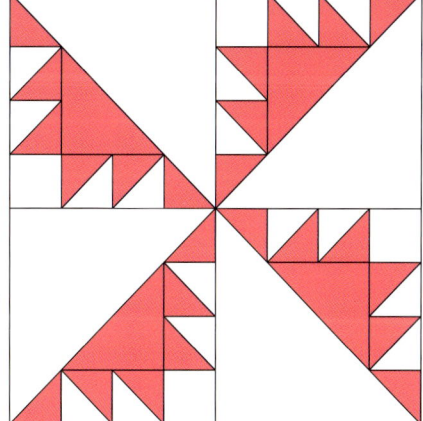

5. Print Half Square Triangulations™ papers. Print 8 copies of page 23 - 2 1/8" finished size.

6. Construct 2 1/8" half square triangles using the 6 ½ " x 9 ½" rectangles **B** of **Background Fabric** with the 6 ½ " x 9 ½" rectangles **K** of **Dark Fabric**. Each rectangle pair will yield twelve half square triangle units measuring 2 5/8" raw edge to raw edge. **Make 84 half square triangle units.** These triangle units will be used for pieced border construction.

Make 2 side border strips with 24 units each.

Make 2 top and bottom border strips using 18 units each.

Quilt Top Assembly

1. Arrange pieced blocks and **Background Fabric** squares and triangles in diagonal rows as diagramed below.

2. Arrange half square triangle units from step 6 to form first border strips, press seams between half square triangle units open. Attach side borders first and then top and bottom borders. Press long seams toward the quilt top.

3. Attach the final border strips. Sides first and then the top and bottom borders. Press toward the final border strips.

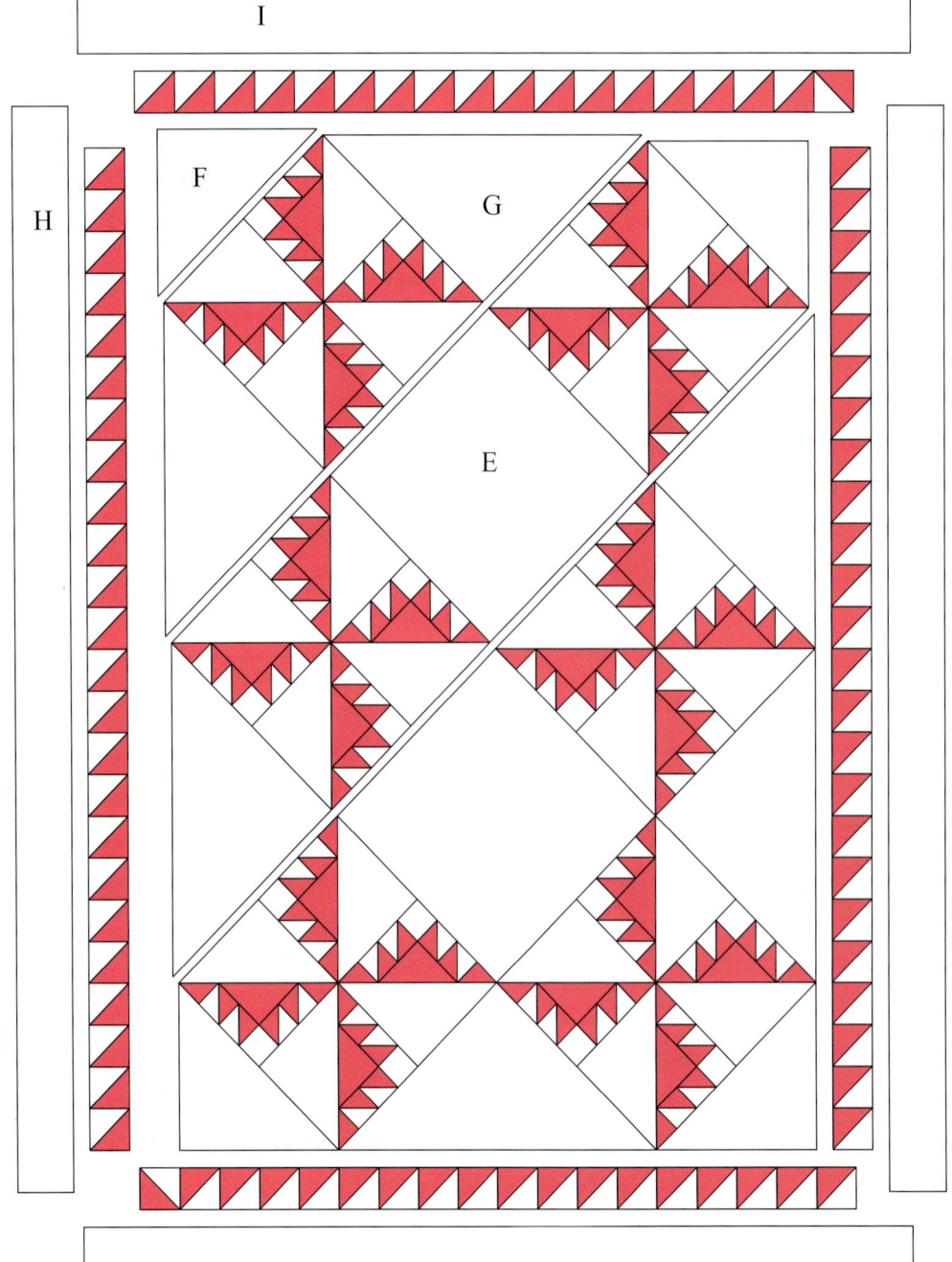

Clown

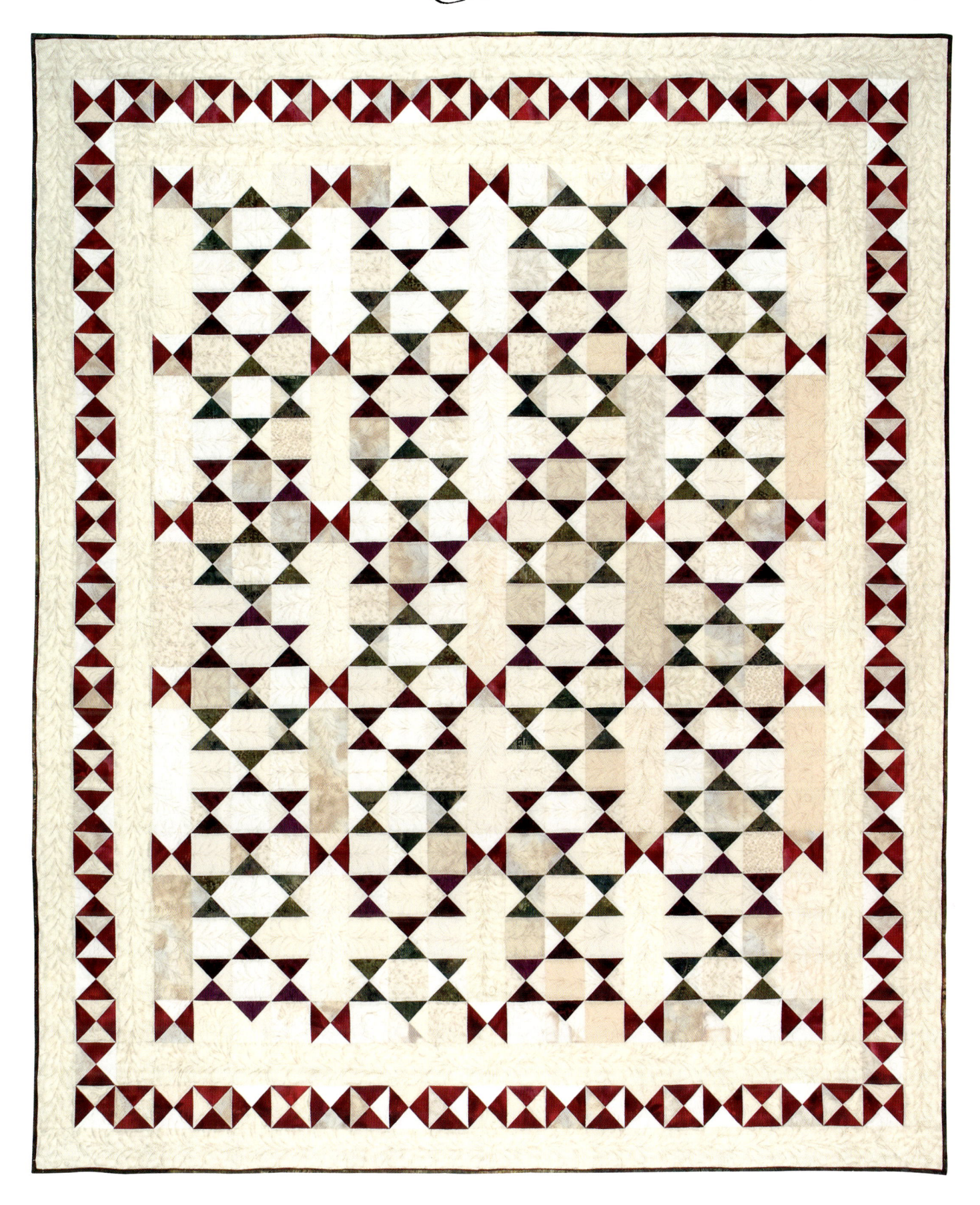

Fabric Requirements and Cutting Instructions:

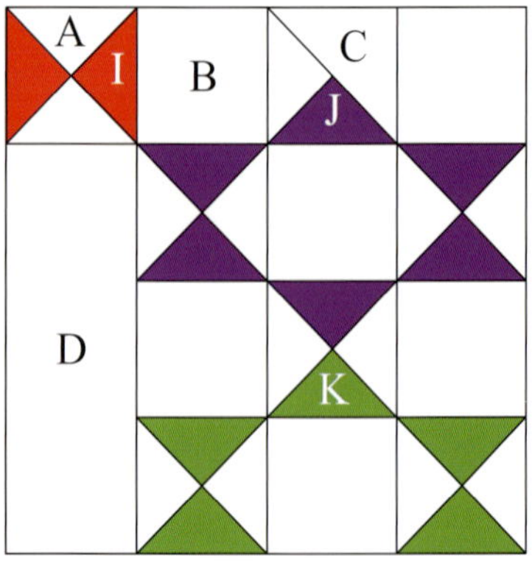

	Twin 76" x 92" 12 - 16" blocks	Queen 92" x 108" 20 - 16" blocks
Background	7 ½ yards	10 yards
A - 8 ½" x 11" rectangles	31	44
B - 4 ½" squares	78	128
C - 4 ⅞" squares — cut once diagonally	3	4
D - 4 ½" x 12 ½" rectangles	16	25
E - First Border - Sides	2 strips 4 ½" x 68 ½"	2 strips 4 ½" x 84 ½"
F - Top and Bottom	2 strips 4 ½" x 60 ½"	2 strips 4 ½" x 76 ½"
G - Final Border - Sides	2 strips 4 ½" x 84 ½"	2 strips 4 ½" x 100 ½"
H - Top and Bottom	2 strips 4 ½" x 76 ½"	2 strips 4 ½" x 92 ½"
Red Fabric	1 ¾ yards	2 yards
I - 8 ½" x 11" rectangles	17	22
Purple Fabric	¾ yard	1 ¼ yards
J - 8 ½" x 11" rectangles	7	11
Green Fabric	1 ½ yards	1 ¾ yards
K - 8 ½" x 11" rectangles	7	11
Binding - 2" strips	9	11
Backing	5 ¾ yards	8 ½ yards

Alternate Cutting for traditional triangle method

Background
A - 5 ¼" squares
  - cut twice diagonally
  Twin: 82   yield: 328 triangles
  Queen: 119   yield: 476 triangles

Red Fabric
I - 5 ¼" squares
  - cut twice diagonally
  Twin: 46   yield: 184 triangles
  Queen: 59   yield: 236 triangles

Purple Fabric
J - 5 ¼" squares
  - cut twice diagonally
  Twin: 18   yield: 72 triangles
  Queen: 30   yield: 120 triangles

Green Fabric
K - 5 ¼" squares
  - cut twice diagonally
  Twin: 18   yield: 72 triangles
  Queen: 30   yield: 120 triangles

Block Construction

1. **Print Quarter Square Triangulations™ papers. Print page 36 - 4" finished size.**

Print	Twin	31 copies
	Queen	44 copies

2. Construct 4" quarter square triangles using the 8 ½" x 11" rectangles **A** of **Background Fabric** with the rectangles **I** of **Red Fabric**, rectangles **J** of **Purple Fabric** and rectangles **K** of **Green Fabric**. Each rectangle pair will yield eleven quarter square triangle units.

3. Stitch triangle pairs from step 2 together to create hour glass blocks. Make hour glass units as directed below.

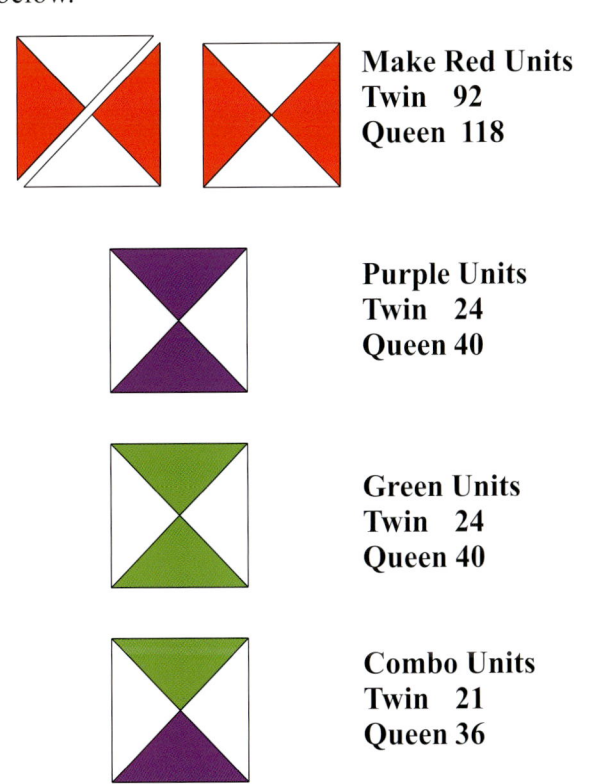

Make Red Units
Twin 92
Queen 118

Purple Units
Twin 24
Queen 40

Green Units
Twin 24
Queen 40

Combo Units
Twin 21
Queen 36

4. Pull the last two or three stitches of the vertical seams that extend past the long seam into the 1/4" seam allowance. This will allow you to split the long seam at the center; all of the seams will be rotating in the same direction and the bulk at the center will be distributed. The hour glass blocks measure 4 ½" raw edge to raw edge.

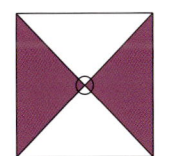

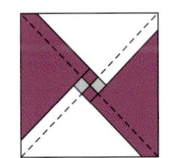

5. Join the remaining green and purple **quarter square units** to the **Background Fabric** triangles **C**. Press toward **C**.

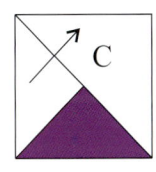

Make Purple Units
Twin 3
Queen 4

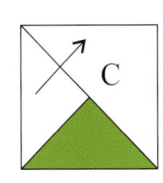

Make Green Units
Twin 3
Queen 4

6. Stitch the block units together as diagramed below. Press all seams open to reduce bulk. Blocks will measure 16 ½" raw edge to raw edge. Border units will measure 4 ½" x 16 ½" raw edge to raw edge.

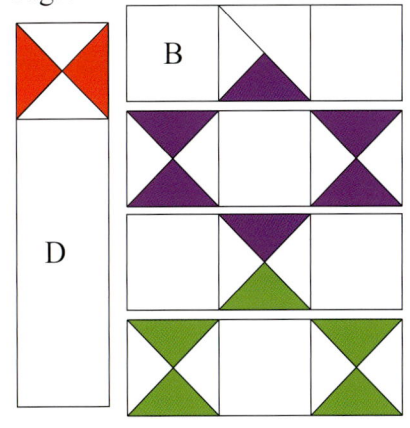

Make Upper Row Blocks
Twin 3
Queen 4

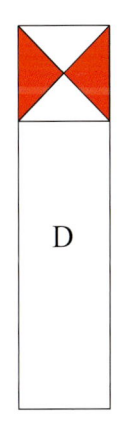

Make Right Border
Twin 4
Queen 5

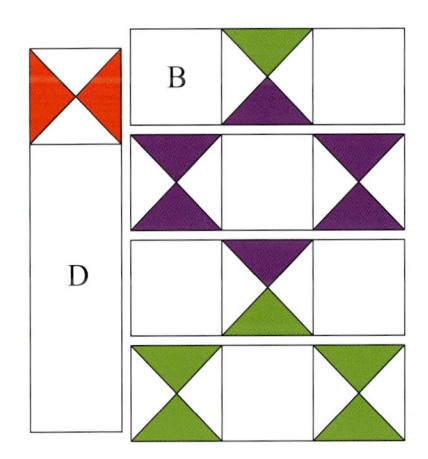

Make
Twin 9
Queen 16

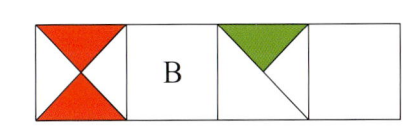

Make Bottom Border
Twin 3
Queen 4

Quilt Top Assembly

1. Arrange the blocks and border units in rows. Pay close attention to the placement as diagramed below. Stitch rows together. Press all seams open to reduce bulk.

2. Apply first border strips. Attach side borders first and then the top and bottom borders. Press all seams toward the border strips.

3. Join remaining red hour glass units together to form pieced border strips. Seams can be pressed open to reduce bulk. **Make 2 of each border strip**.

Side Borders
Twin	19 units
Queen	23 units

Top and Bottom Borders
Twin	17 units
Queen	21 units

4. Attach side borders first, and then top and bottom borders. Press toward the first border strips.

5. Apply final border strips. Attach side borders first and then the top and bottom borders. Press all seams toward the final border strips.

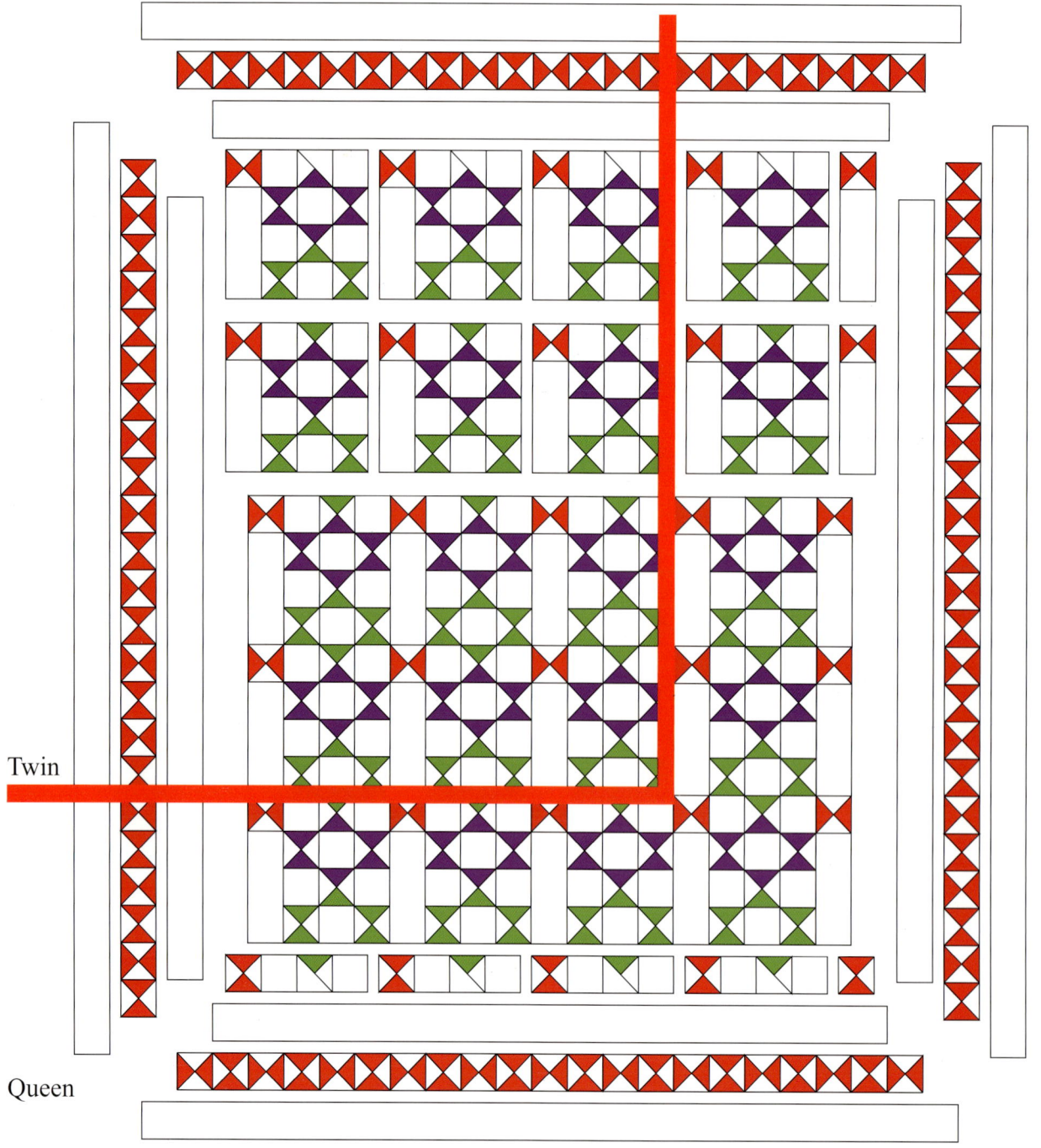

Twin

Queen

Trip to the Altar

Fabric Requirements and Cutting Instructions:

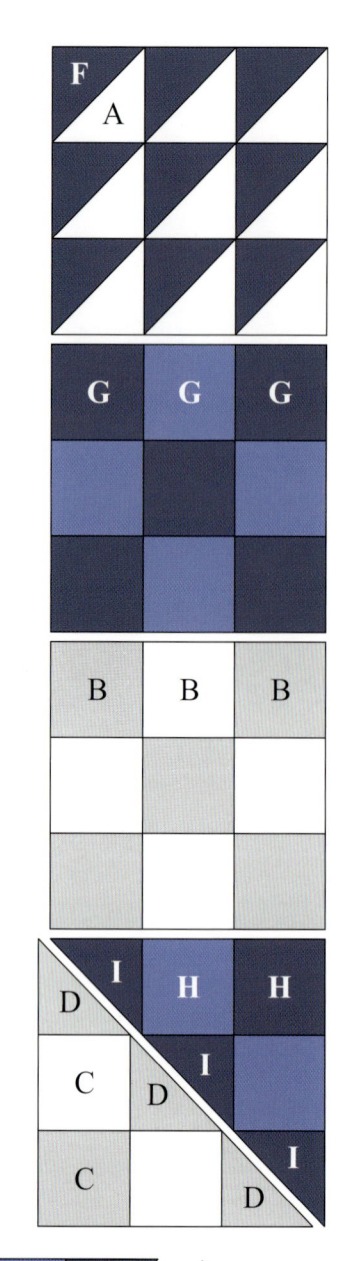

	Twin 76 1/2" x 89" 72 - 9" blocks	Queen 89" x 102" 98 - 9" blocks
Assorted White Fabrics	5 ¾ yards	7 ¼ yards
A - 8 ¼" squares	48	63
B - 3 ½" strips	15 strips	18 strips
C - 3 ½" squares	18	41
D - 6 ¼" squares - cut twice diagonally	5	11
E - 3 ¾" square - cut once diagonally	0	1 square
Assorted Blue Fabrics	6 yards	7 ¾ yards
F - 8 ¼" squares	48	63
G - 3 ½" strips	9 strips	18 strips
H - 3 ½" squares	52	41
I - 6 ¼" squares - cut twice diagonally	14	11
J - 3 ¾" square - cut once diagonally	2	1
Binding - 2" strips	9	10
Backing	5 ½ yards	8 yards

Alternate Cutting for traditional triangle method

Background
  A - 3 7/8" squares
    - cut once diagonally   189   252
              yield: 378 triangles   yield: 504 triangles
Blue
  F - 3 7/8" squares
    - cut once diagonally   189   252
              yield: 378 triangles   yield: 504 triangles

Triangle Block Construction

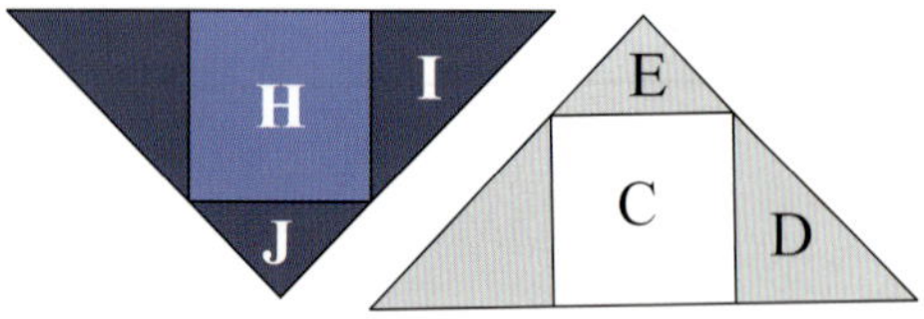

1. **Print Half Square Triangulations™ papers.**
   Print page 30 - 3" finished size.

   Print   Twin   48 copies
   **   Queen   63 copies**

2. Construct half square triangles, place a 8 ¼" square **A** of **Background Fabric** right sides together with rectangle **F** of **Dark Fabric**. Construct half square triangles following the Triangulations™ paper method. Each square pair will yield eight half square triangle units measuring 3 ½" raw edge to raw edge. Repeat using all **A** and **F** squares.

   Make   Twin   378
   **   Queen   504**

3. Arrange the half square triangles into rows as diagramed below. Press the seams as indicated by the arrows.

   Make   **Twin   42 blocks**
              Queen   56 blocks

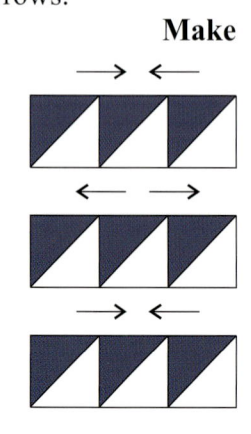

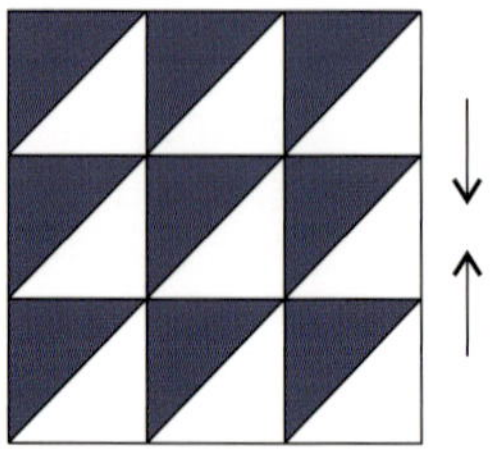

44

Nine Patch Block Construction

1. Stitch 3 ½" wide blue strips together along the long edges. Press the seams toward the center strip.

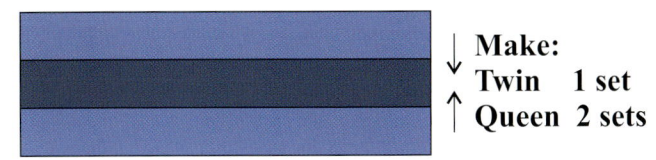

Make:
Twin   1 set
Queen 2 sets

2. Stitch 3 ½" wide blue strips together along the long edges. Press the seams toward the outer strips.

Make:
Twin   2 sets
Queen 4 sets

3. Stitch 3 ½" wide white strips together along the long edges. Press the seams toward the center strip.

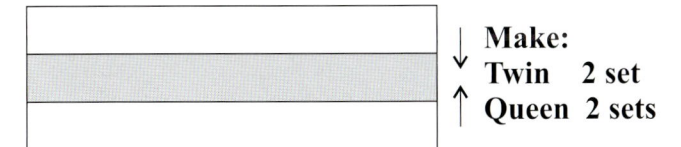

Make:
Twin   2 set
Queen 2 sets

4. Stitch 3 ½" wide white strips together along the long edges. Press the seams toward the outer strips.

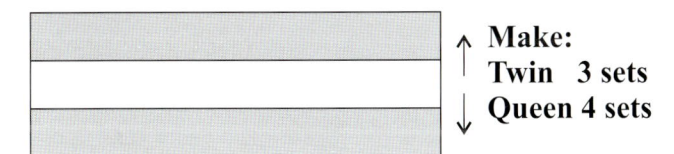

Make:
Twin   3 sets
Queen 4 sets

5. Subcut the strip sets sewn in steps 1 - 4 above. Trim the selvage from the strip ends. Cut the strip sets into 3 ½" segments. Each full strip should yield 12 segments.

Cut Segments: Twin   Queen
  Blue Strip set 1   12   21
  Blue Strip set 2   24   42
  White Strip set 3   18   21
  White Strip set 4   36   42

3 ½" subcut units

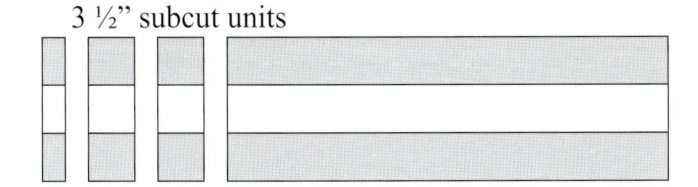

6. Assemble the segments from step 5 into the nine patch blocks diagramed below. Place the segments as shown. Press the seams as indicated by the arrows.

Make Nine Patch Blocks: **Twin**   **Queen**
  Blue   12   21
  White   18   21

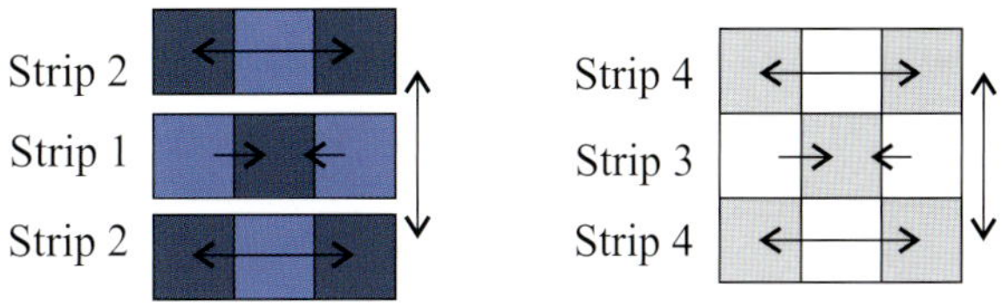

Strip 2 / Strip 1 / Strip 2

Strip 4 / Strip 3 / Strip 4

7. Using the squares and triangles, assemble the setting and corner triangles units diagramed below. Press the seams as indicated by the arrows. The 6 1/4" triangles and 3 3/4" triangles are slightly oversized to allow the squares to "float."

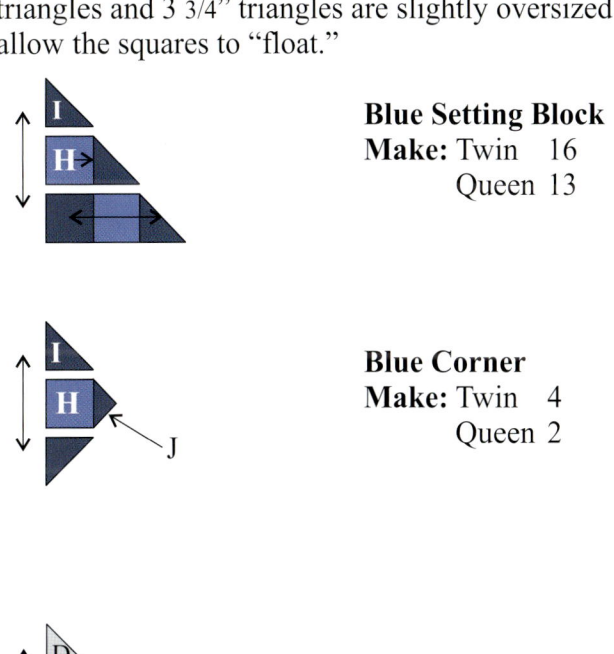

Blue Setting Block
Make: Twin   16
      Queen 13

Blue Corner
Make: Twin   4
      Queen 2

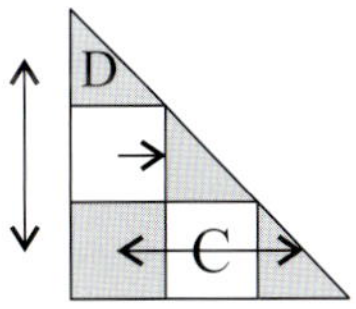

White Setting Block
Make: Twin   6
      Queen 13

White Corner
Make: Twin   0
      Queen 2

Quilt Top Assembly

1. Lay the quilt top out on a floor or design wall. The blocks and triangles are easy to rotate into an incorrect position. Pay close attention to the position of the triangle blocks so as to create the secondary design.

2. The quilt top will be assembled in diagonal rows. Join the blocks and partial blocks together into rows. Press all seams toward the nine patch blocks and the partial blocks.

3. Stitch rows together and press long seams in one direction.

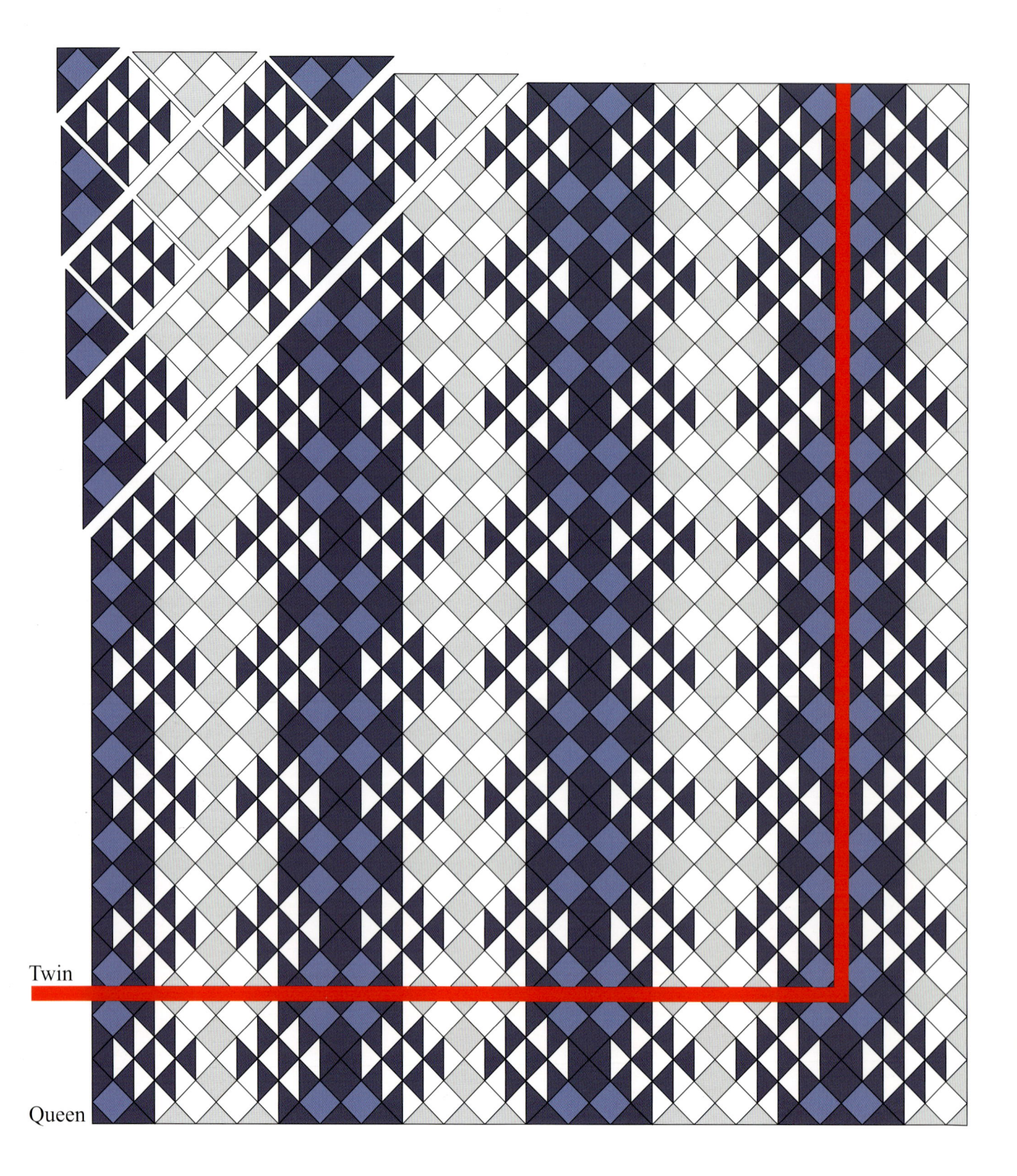

Twin

Queen

Fireworks

Fireworks

Finished Quilt Size:
79 1/4" x 90 1/2" plus border width of choice

All of the fabrics shown at the right are Hoffman Bali Batiks. The corresponding Hoffman style and color numbers are provided to aid in your fabric collection.

Alternate Cutting for traditional triangle method

Fabric 1
- 2 squares 4 1/2"
- 2 squares 5 1/4"

Fabric 2
- 13 squares 4 1/2"
- 12 squares 5 1/4"

Fabric 3
- 20 squares 4 1/2"
- 20 squares 5 1/4"

Fabric 4
- 28 squares 4 1/2"
- 28 squares 5 1/4"

Fabric 5
- 36 squares 4 1/2"
- 36 squares 5 1/4"

Fabric 6
- 44 squares 4 1/2"
- 44 squares 5 1/4"

Fabric 7
- 52 squares 4 1/2"
- 52 squares 5 1/4"

Fabric 8
- 14 squares 7"
- 2 squares 4 7/8"
- 28 squares 5 1/4"

Cut all 5 1/4" squares twice diagonally.
Use 5 1/4" quarter square triangles to make hour glass units as listed on page 49.

Fabric Requirements and Cutting Instructions:

Fabric 1   1 fat quarter
- 1895-382 Grape Juice
- 2 squares 4 1/2"
- 2 rectangles 8 1/2" x 11"

Fabric 2   1 yard
- S839-130 Multi
- 13 squares 4 1/2"
- 5 rectangles 8 1/2" x 11"

Fabric 3   1 1/4 yards
- 1895-381 Pomegranate
- 20 squares 4 1/2"
- 8 rectangles 8 1/2" x 11"

Fabric 4   1 3/4 yards
- D167-263 Shrimp
- 28 squares 4 1/2"
- 11 rectangles 8 1/2" x 11"

Fabric 5   2 yards
- 884-97 Raspberry
- 36 squares 4 1/2"
- 14 rectangles 8 1/2" x 11"

Fabric 6   2 1/4 yards
- E130-212 Berry
- 44 squares 4 1/2"
- 17 rectangles 8 1/2" x 11"

Fabric 7   2 1/2 yards
- 1895-382 Grape Juice
- 52 squares 4 1/2"
- 20 rectangles 8 1/2" x 11"

Fabric 8   1 3/4 yards
- D164-97 Raspberry
- 14 squares 7"
- 2 squares 4 7/8"
- 11 rectangles 8 1/2" x 11"

optional border   2 3/4 yards
binding   1 yard

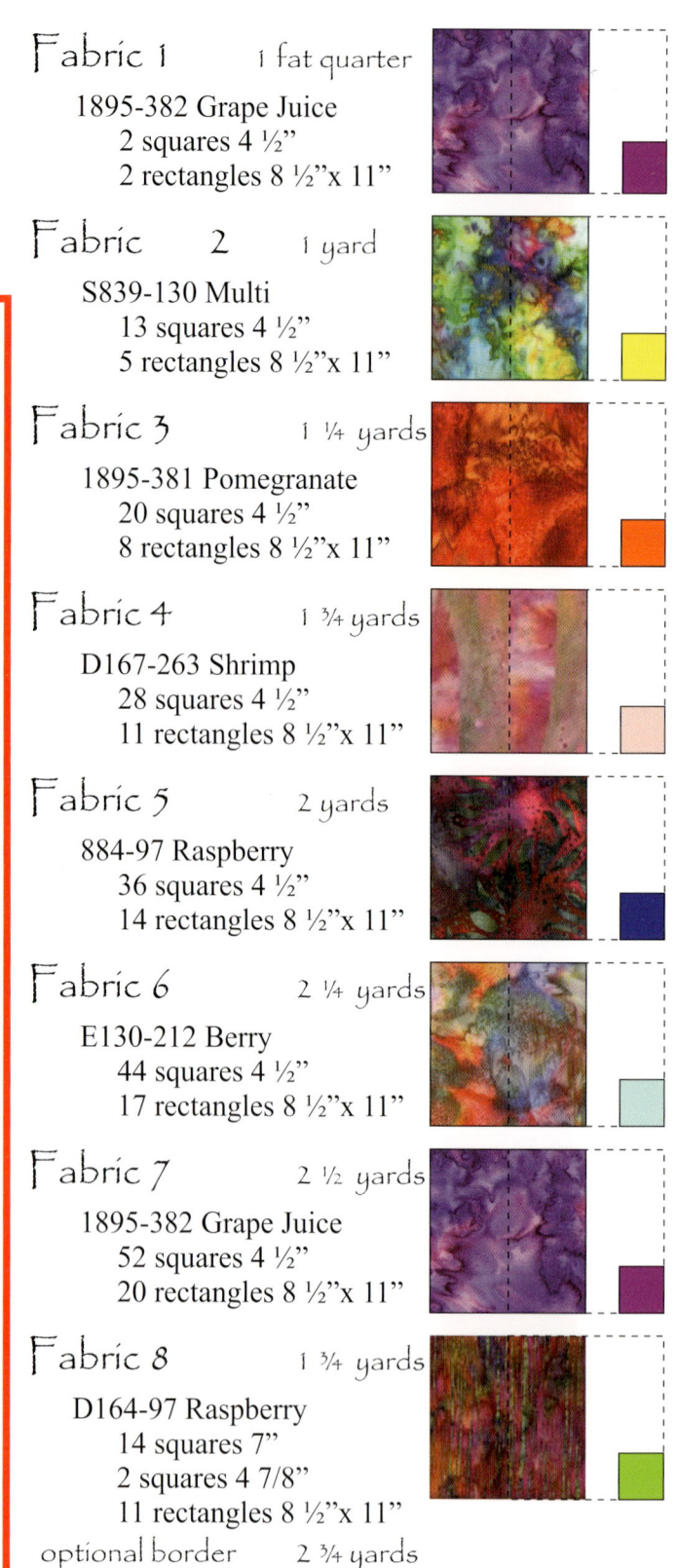

Backing

5-1/2 yards without optional final border

9 yards with optional border

Cut 3/4" swatches of fabrics 1-8 and adhere to the squares. This will help you keep the fabrics in order.

Quarter Square Triangle Construction

1. Print Quarter Square Triangulations™ papers. Print 44 copies of page 36 - 4" finished size.

2. Construct quarter square triangles using the fabric combinations diagramed at right. Place two 8 ½" x 11" rectangles of fabric right sides together. Construct quarter square triangles following the Triangulations™ paper method. Each rectangle pair will yield eleven quarter square triangle units.

3. Stitch triangle pairs from step 2 together to create hour glass blocks.

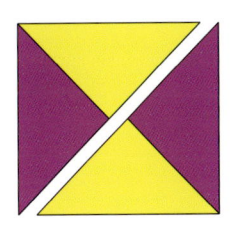

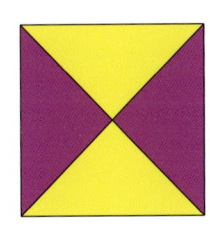

4. Pull the last two or three stitches of the vertical seams that extend past the long seam into the 1/4" seam allowance. This will allow you to split the long seam at the center, all of the seams will be rotating in the same direction and the bulk at the center will be distributed. The hour glass blocks measure 4 ½".

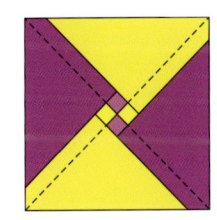

5. Cut each 7" square of Fabric 8 twice diagonally to create quarter square triangles, to be placed along the sides of the quilt.

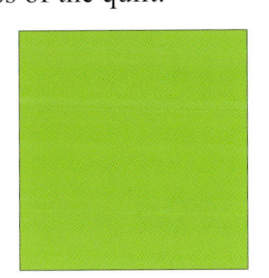

7. Cut each 4 7/8" square of Fabric 8 once diagonally to create half square triangles for the quilt corners.

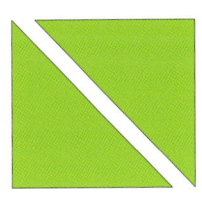

Unit A - Fabrics 1 and 2
Stitch 2 rectangle pairs
Need 8 hour glass blocks

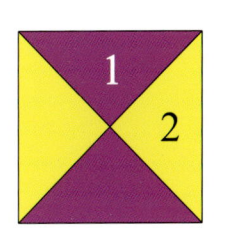

Unit B - Fabrics 2 and 3
Stitch 3 rectangle pairs
Need 16 hour glass blocks

Unit C - Fabrics 3 and 4
Stitch 5 rectangle pairs
Need 24 hour glass blocks

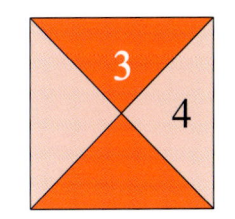

Unit D - Fabrics 4 and 5
Stitch 6 rectangle pairs
Need 32 hour glass blocks

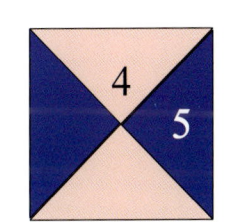

Unit E - Fabrics 5 and 6
Stitch 8 rectangle pairs
Need 40 hour glass blocks

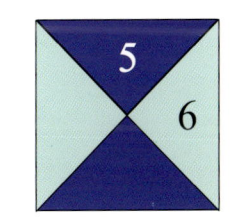

Unit F - Fabrics 6 and 7
Stitch 9 rectangle pairs
Need 48 hour glass blocks

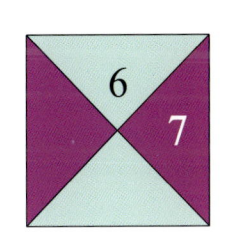

Unit G - Fabrics 7 and 8
Stitch 11 rectangle pairs
Need 56 hour glass blocks

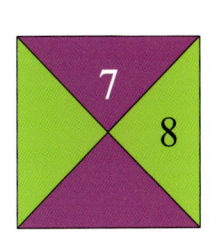

Quilt Top Arrangement

It is helpful to arrange the units on a large floor or design wall to ensure that the proper position of the quarter square triangles is maintained. If the quarter square triangles are turned incorrectly, the "star point" will disappear.

You may choose to start the arrangement from the center of the quilt, working toward the outer edge. Place the first three plain squares of fabric...two squares of **Fabric 1** and one square of **Fabric 2**. Arrange hour glass blocks **A** around the three squares, pay careful attention to the placement of the hour glass blocks which will create the star points as diagramed.

Place the next round of **Fabric 2** squares, and then the round of **B hour glass blocks**. Continue adding rounds of plain squares and hour glass blocks. The final round of fabric pieces added will be the **Fabric 8 half and quarter square triangles.**

Quilt Top Construction

The quilt top is constructed in diagonal rows.

Starting at a corner, join the units in rows as diagramed.

It is helpful to place the plain squares in such a way as to take advantage of the grain of the fabric. I have found it best to place the non-stretchy, lengthwise grain of the fabric parallel to the seams when assembling the rows. Gently stretch the fabric vertically and horizontally to determine which has the least stretch. This will allow you to use the stretchier crosswise grain of the fabric to ease any piecing differences when joining the rows together.

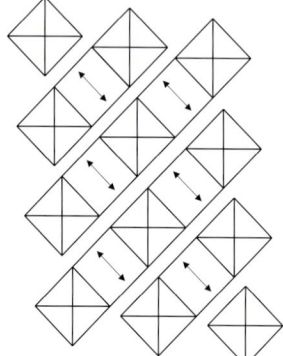

Stitch the units together into rows. Press all seams toward the plain squares.

Stitch the rows together. Press the long seams toward the center of the quilt.

Cut final border strips as desired. The model quilt was bordered with 10 ½" wide strips. Strips were cut on the lengthwise grain to minimize stretching of the edge. Apply side borders first and then top and bottom borders. Press seams toward the border strips.